OUR PLUS ONE

MONTH-TO-MONTH GUIDE FOR RAISING A
NEWBORN BABY FROM BIRTH TO 6 MONTHS

ELIZABETH NEWBOURNE

CONTENTS

14 Baby Essentials Every Mom Must Have...

This checklist includes:

- 14 ESSENTIALS THAT YOU DIDN'T KNOW YOU NEEDED FOR YOUR LITTLE ONE AND YOURSELF
- ITEMS WHICH WILL MAKE BEING A MAMA BEAR EASIER
- WHERE YOU CAN PURCHASE THESE ITEMS AT THE LOWEST PRICE

The last thing you want to do is be unprepared and unequipped to give your little one an enjoyable and secure environment to grow up in. It is never too late to prepare for this!

To receive your free Mommy Checklist, visit the link or scan the QR code below:

https://purelypublishing.activehosted.com/f/1

Well done! You grew a tiny human inside your tummy for nine months and now have a warm, soft, and sweet-smelling baby to cradle in your arms. I know you may have said goodbye to the nausea, heartburn, swollen feet, and constantly aching back that come with pregnancy, but the worry that started from the first moment you saw you were pregnant is still with you. That is perfectly normal. You have this precious life in your hands, and you and your partner want to be the best possible parents.

There is a lot of information out there, and deciding which book, article, or blog post takes the best approach is tiresome. The last thing you need is something else to drain away the little energy you have left. Taking care of your little bundle of joy isn't always so joyous—late-night feedings, no sleep, a crying baby, and changing diaper after diaper take a toll on a person.

I want to help make your life easier and share with you everything you need to know about caring for your baby in the first six months and show you how you and your partner can take care of yourselves. I know you both are so focused on giving your baby everything they need, you end up neglecting your health and relationship. This isn't healthy, and striking a balance is paramount to the long-term happiness of your little family.

If I'm honest, my husband and I went through a rough patch after giving birth to our first child. I put on the 'mom' hat and completely forgot that I'm more than that. I'm a wife also. It was during this time when I realized that a lot of books focus mostly on the baby and not so much on the family unit. I can tell you that having some on-hand guidance while trying to navigate being a new mom and maintaining a healthy relationship with my partner would have been a tremendous help. We were able to see a relationship counselor, and she gave us the tools to be good parents while being caring partners. But not everyone has the luxury of seeing a professional for help. Luckily, now I am fortunate enough to be able to share these tips and tricks with you so that you don't experience the hopelessness we did.

Once I've convinced you that your health and happiness will lead to you being a better parent, we'll move on to how to feed your baby and what milestones they will reach in their first six months. Each month of your little one's life up until month six will have its own chapter to make it easy for you to turn to if you need to look something up. I want *Our Plus One* to be your very own baby instruction manual!

But even after soaking up all the information you can about your baby's first six months, I want you to remember that you always have a second chance to do things right. No book can prepare you for the days you forget to pack extra diapers or an extra set of baby clothes in case of an unfortunate wet burp. You will need to learn how to roll with these mistakes, learn from them, and move on. Tomorrow is another day, and you'll pack five extra diapers just in case.

I remember there were days where I thought I had finally figured things out, then the next day I'd be back at square one. Putting my daughter to sleep is a good example. As soon as I figured out she wanted to be swaddled before going to sleep, she changed and preferred the sleep sack instead. At first, each change made me feel like I let her down in some way, but as I got used to my little princess and how her needs transitioned, it became easier to look at it as a part of her growth and not a failure on my part. Moms may be superheroes, but we can't read minds. While you won't develop mommy intuition overnight, if you know what to expect, you may have a more stress-free experience.

It is my goal to share with you all the experience I gained through my three pregnancies, as well as what I learned through my years as a nutritionist working with new moms. I care deeply about being a trusted source of information for you during this time because I wish I had someone who understood what

I was going through and could guide me through all my pregnancies. Yes, all my pregnancies because each one came with its own challenges. So, whether you're a new mom or just gave birth to your second or third munchkin, I can help.

Let's get started. I know you can't wait to read about all the milestones your little bug will go through in the next six months. And just so you know, it's not going overboard when you record and celebrate every change that takes place!

BABY IN THE HOUSE!

There are a few things you will have to do before you bring your baby home. If you do this, you will feel more relaxed about the tiny new family member in the house, and you will be able to cope with mental stressors.

Before we look at how mommy can look after her mental health, let's look at preparing everything for your baby.

KEEPING YOUR BABY SAFE

It's a blessing to be a parent, but it doesn't come without its challenges. I know I saw everything as a danger in the first few months of my baby's life.

Actually, if I'm honest, that never goes away, but by focusing on a few key areas, you'll be able to relieve some of the worries you will feel as a mother.

1. Crib Safety

When you buy your baby's crib, you must make sure it meets safety standards. There are also specific things you should avoid when you put your baby down for a nap to prevent sudden infant death syndrome (Mayo Clinic, n.d.).

When shopping for the perfect crib, keep the following in mind:

- The space between each slat should be no more than 2⅜ inches to ensure your baby can't fit through. You can use a soda can to measure and make sure the space is safe. It goes without saying that you should not use a crib with any missing or cracked slats.
- Make sure that all screws, brackets, and hardware are installed securely and no parts of the crib are missing.
- Corner posts should not be higher than 1/16 inch to ensure that no parts of the baby's clothing get caught.

- There shouldn't be any cut-outs or holes in the headboard where your little one's head can get stuck.

For your baby's safety, when placed in the crib, make sure to:

- Place your baby on their back on a firm, tight-fitting mattress.
- Remove any pillows, comforters, bumper pads, and pillow-like stuffed toys from the crib.
- Use a sleeper instead of a blanket. If you do use a blanket, tuck the blanket under the mattress and only cover your baby as high as their chest.
- Use a fitted sheet made explicitly for the crib.

2. Car Seat

Probably one of the most important and first things you must do is get a car seat. It is not legal or safe to transport your baby from the hospital any other way than in a secure car seat.

. . .

When you install the seat, make sure it does not face the front of the car. Since your little one's head is disproportionate to their body, the chances of spinal cord and neck injuries increase should an accident take place and the seat is forward-facing. It is recommended that you keep your child in a rear-facing car seat until one year of age or 20 pounds.

3. Co-Sleeping

As a new mommy, I know you want to keep your little one as close as possible, even while you're sleeping. There are pros to co-sleeping, but you have to consider that there is the risk of you or your partner rolling on top of them and suffocating them. I suggest putting the crib next to your bed. This way you'll have your baby close by, and there won't be any risk.

4. Changing Table

When buying a changing table, make sure it has a sturdy surface with a guardrail on all sides. The middle should be lower to make sure your baby stays in one place. You can also get one with a safety strap to ensure that they don't fall.

. . .

5. Staircase

If you have a staircase in your house, you have to make sure that you restrict your child's access by using a baby gate or a fence. Babies go through a lot of changes during the first six months, and you may be surprised to find your child approaching the staircase and not playing with their toys where you left them. You may only turn around for a second, and an accident may happen. Protect your tiny one from danger.

6. Pets

Before your baby arrived, you probably treated your pets like a part of the family. There's no need for you to change this, but you have to take some safety precautions. It is estimated that 51% of dog bite victims are children (Kids n K-9s, n.d.). To prevent any accidents from happening, don't leave your baby alone with the family pet. It would be best if you also teach your children from a young age to be gentle with animals.

7. Your Television

You'd be surprised to learn that approximately ten children die each year due to falling TVs (CPSC,

2012). It may be good for you to consider mounting your flat screen or, at the very least, securing your TV to the cabinet with a TV anchor. I suggest you also have a look at other pieces of furniture or appliances that you will need to baby-proof.

8. The Fireplace

You should not use your fireplace if it has not been baby-proofed. It doesn't matter if it is a wood- or gas-burning fireplace; you need to find an effective way to restrict your baby's access to it. I always placed my little ones in a fenced-in area when we used the fireplace on chilly nights.

9. Electrical Outlets

It's evident that a baby's safety was not kept in mind when electrical outlets were designed. Those holes beg curious little fingers to poke and prod. According to the National Fire Protection Association, close to 2,400 children suffer from burns and severe shocks each year (n.d.). The easiest and most cost-effective way to baby-proof electrical outlets is by using caps or plugs.

. . .

10. Corner Safety

As your baby learns to walk, you can expect quite a few falls, making pointed corners one of the areas you cannot neglect when it comes to safety. Walk through your home and look for any areas you can soften up. This includes sharp edges on tables and couches. You can buy furniture padding that will protect your bundle of joy's head and body should they fall, and it won't look unsightly.

11. Doors

Even as adults, we sometimes still get our fingers caught in the door, so we know just how much it hurts. To protect your child from this hazard, buy some pinch guards, and there won't be any unnecessary tears.

The above 11 areas are some of the most important things to focus on when you prepare your home for the baby's arrival. But what about other little ones who will now have to share mommy and daddy with another tiny human? If you have any other children, there are a few ways you can get them just as excited about their new brother or sister as you are.

AVOID SIBLING RIVALRY

It is difficult for most children to deal with the fact that there will be a new family member with whom they now have to share their space and, especially, their parents. If your child is older, they may even show some aggression. In some instances, you may even notice that they start acting more like a baby, asking to drink out of a bottle or wetting themselves.

You have to prepare your child for this massive change by telling them what they should expect. Also, try your best to reassure them that they won't be losing anything but gaining a new friend and play-mate. Keep in mind that this is one of the most challenging things your child will have to deal with, and after the new baby arrives, you will have to make some changes to make the adjustment easier.

As I mentioned before, I have three kids, so I had to go through this process twice—and so did my eldest. I'd like to say that the second time was better for him, but unfortunately, it was worse. If you're bringing a third baby into this world, you will have to pay a little extra attention to your first-born and be there for your middle child.

Here are some things you can do to prepare your child for their new sibling:

- Tell them that you're expecting another child as soon as possible. They should hear this important news from you and not someone else.
- If the older child needs to move to a new room or changes need to be made to their current space to accommodate the new baby, do so well in advance. You don't want to make any major changes once your baby arrives because you don't want the older child to feel displaced.
- Find out if there are any sibling preparation classes in your area. I also found it helped when I took my children on a hospital tour to set their minds at ease.

Don't forget to stop to look at the new babies!

- Take your child with you to your prenatal appointments. Make them part of the process as much as possible.
- Be honest about what your child can expect after you bring their sibling home. Tell them that you will be tired, and the new baby will take a lot of your time in the beginning. Explain to them that newborns can't do anything for themselves yet, and you both will need to help them. Also, make it clear that although their new sibling won't be their playmate, in a few months, that will change.
- If you have any friends with a new baby, visit them if possible.
- Read your child books about pregnancy and newborns. Answer any questions or concerns they may have. Allow them to vent any feelings that may be triggered by the books.
- Watch any baby videos you have of your older child growing up, starting with them as a baby. Talk about how excited you were when they were born.

- Let your child practice how to hold a doll and support the head. Teach them to be gentle.
- Include your child when you're picking your new baby's coming-home outfit.

When your new family member is home safe and sound, you will have to put in some extra effort. I know you'll be tired, but you must do your best for your older child to accept the new bundle of joy in the house. This includes:

- **Making time for the older child.** Set aside time to spend one-on-one time together. Even just 10 minutes of uninterrupted time can mean the world to your older child. It will also help curb any negative behavior that may arise from having to share you with another baby.
- **Listening.** When your child expresses any negative feelings about their new sibling, acknowledge them. Don't ever deny your child's feelings; instead, help them voice their feelings.
- **Expressing feelings.** Help your child

with ways to express any angry feelings they may have toward their little brother or sister. You can tell them to draw an angry picture, roar like a lion, or shout into a pillow. You want them to take any possible aggression out on anything other than the baby.

- **Creating space.** Give your older child their own private space and things they do not have to share with their sibling.
- **If your child wants to help with the baby's care, let them.**

MOMMY'S RECOVERY

You may have forgotten how it feels to take care of yourself. Even throughout your pregnancy, self-care may have been last on your to-do list (even though it is very important). With a new baby in the house, self-care will be pushed to the back of your mind even more. After all, where will you get the time when your baby needs your attention most of the day? Between changing diapers, nursing your baby, and interrupted sleep, you're going to be exhausted and overwhelmed, and just sitting down on the couch for a split second will be a blessing.

I know a lot of new mothers say they hardly get time to eat; I even struggled to get enough time to take a shower!

It was only after my second child that I realized how essential it was to consider my well-being.

You have to keep in mind that raising a child is a full-time job, and you deserve a rest too. Here are my top five tips to practice self-care when you're a mommy:

- **Rest when your little one does:** Some moms can't sleep when their baby is sleeping, but that doesn't mean you can't get some sort of rest in. Don't go on a cleaning spree when baby is catching some z's; instead, make yourself a cup of tea and sit down on the couch. You can even take this time to read a book or listen to a podcast. Do anything that will make you unwind and relax.
- **Get active:** Okay, I know this sounds contradictory to what I just said, but there is a difference between moving your body

while mopping the floor and going for a walk in the sun and fresh air. If you don't have someone to look after your baby so that you can go outdoors, yoga is a good way to get your blood pumping and relax you in one go.

- **Build community:** In my previous book, *Table for Two*, I took a lot of time to explain why community is so important during pregnancy. The same can be said after giving birth. Stay-at-home mommies often feel isolated since they are cooped up alone all day. The best thing you can do for yourself is to find a community of support. Other moms are a good source of support, as are Facebook community buddies. I widened my circle of friends a lot by introducing myself to mothers at the play park and by joining Facebook groups for new moms. Start making connections while you're still pregnant; this will make it easier after giving birth.

- **Be mindful:** Focusing on the special moments will ground you. What sounds is your little one making, how do they smell, how does it feel to hold their tiny hands between yours? While doing this, take deep breaths and relax into them. You'll feel more serene in a split second.

- **Ask and accept help:** It doesn't matter if it's your spouse, friend, neighbor, mother-in-law, or even a therapist—when you need help, ask for it. After giving birth, there will be a lot of caring people around you, and they will often ask you if you need anything. Be honest and tell them what you need. You deserve help during this time, and you do not have to do it alone.

I know that taking time away from your baby will be tough. Keep telling yourself that it is the quality of time you spend with them that is important, not the quantity. If you feel tired and stressed out, you have to take care of yourself before you can care for anyone else. Still don't believe me? Here are some reasons why you should take time to fill your cup:

- Taking care of yourself maintains your sense of self-worth.
- You will set a good example for your kids if you practice self-care.
- You can become physically sick and suffer

from burnout if you don't rest.

- When your body is depleted, you're more likely to get sick.
- You can become emotionally unwell; depression and anxiety are often caused by burnout.

All in all, self-care shouldn't be seen as a luxury but a necessity for you and your baby.

DON'T FORGET ABOUT YOUR PARTNER

Dirty diapers, crying, fatigue, mood swings—doesn't sound very romantic, does it? The fact is babies make even the most straightforward tasks difficult, not to mention maintaining a relationship. There's this romantic notion that a bouncing bundle of joy will enrich you and your partner's life considerably. Although that is true in the most basic sense of receiving unconditional love from this tiny little human, there's more to it.

If you want to keep your marriage or relationship healthy after giving birth, communication is key. It is something you should start working on long before your baby enters this world. I found the best way to work on communication is to include each other in all decisions surrounding pregnancy, birth, and upbringing. It is especially beneficial to the partner who is not carrying the baby. It's easy to feel left out when mommy goes through the physical changes and makes all the decisions.

To help couples prepare for a new family member, there are parental relationship courses to teach mom and dad what they can realistically expect when they become parents. These courses explain how the relationship dynamic will change once the baby arrives.

It often happens that you both end up showering your newborn with so much love that you forget about each other. But I want you to realize that looking after your relationship with your partner is just as important as nurturing your baby. Remember that your baby will grow up seeing and feeling the bond you have with your significant other, so you must make an effort to keep the love alive. Another way to look at it is this: Your baby won't stay little forever but will grow up and leave home, but your partner will stay behind with you.

I realize that keeping the flame burning is difficult when you're faced with diapers, dirty bottles, and piles of laundry. At its core, the solution is spending quality time together. Here are some tips on how you can strengthen your relationship after baby arrives.

Common ground: Before you even get pregnant, you and your partner should have had a discussion to make sure both of you are ready for this big step. If you both decide to have a child, there is a bigger chance that the little one can play a positive role in your relationship and bring you closer together.

However, if one of you isn't on board with the idea of having a baby, it could be detrimental to your marriage.

Keep your expectations in check: Parenthood isn't as glamorous as some movies make it out to be. It is crucial for you as a couple to talk to other parents to determine how the baby affected their relationship. Raising children is going to be the biggest job of your life, so it is a good idea to get some tips and tricks to succeed not just as a parent but as a unit.

Communicate: You and your partner need to talk about what you expect from each other as parents and partners. For example, if mom expects dad to take charge of 50% of everything child-related but dad believes that it's 100% mom's duty, there will be trouble. Negotiate something that will work for both of you. But most of all, be honest to avoid any future issues.

Mind-reading skills: Often, we believe that our partners should instinctively know what we want, sometimes even before we know ourselves! This is an unfair expectation that will put unnecessary strain on your relationship. You may think, why doesn't my partner take care of the baby for an hour after they get home from work? Well, probably because you didn't let them know that you expect them to. This is part of the previous point: communication. You should be brave enough to explain what you need and why. Constant communication will strengthen your relationship in the long run.

Really listen: There will be times when your partner comes to you with a problem. Since you love them, you may want to try and solve that problem. But that is not always why your partner is telling you about the issue. Sometimes they just want someone to listen and be supportive. As an example, when you tell your husband that you're frustrated because the little one has been crying the whole day, you don't really want advice, do you? It's more a case of your partner being understanding and sympathetic than trying to fix it. Listen, and only give advice when they outright ask for it.

Tag-team: It's easy to get cranky and take it out on your partner when you haven't had a good night's sleep in a while, especially during the first few months. To lessen the strain on one person, take turns to look after the baby during the night. My partner and I took turns. One night, he'd get up when our baby cried; the other night was my turn. This really kept the irritability at bay and prevented us from snapping at each other at the breakfast table. Find a sleep schedule that works for both of you; some couples tag-team two nights and not one. It all depends on you.

Top priority: I know when you have a new baby in the house, they will be your main priority. However, this is something you should guard against. You can't put your relationship on the back burner, and then 20 years later, when your kid moves out, expect it to bounce back. Couple care is essential. To keep the flame burning, think of having a date night each week, or maybe put your little one to sleep an hour earlier to give you some adult time. As I mentioned before, it's not just for your benefit to be a happy couple; it's good for your child too.

IT TAKES A VILLAGE

I briefly touched on having a support system earlier in this chapter, and I cannot overstate the importance of having people to help you. When you have someone to encourage you and help you through your pregnancy and after giving birth, you will feel less stressed, which means your baby will be more relaxed too.

Close to half of new parents feel they lack support when they feel somewhat stressed out (Zero to Three, 2016). This is why it is crucial for you to start to build your support system as early as possible. Take it as seriously as all other preparations you're making for after your baby's birth.

Family

You and your partner's siblings, parents, grandparents, and other family members can take a lot of the pressure off, which will improve your overall well-being. They can compensate in any areas where you may be falling behind, such as doing laundry, prepping a meal, or even offering some advice. Research shows that children grow up to be more resilient when everyone in their family lends a hand raising them (Chen et al., 2017).

Friends

I don't know what I would've done without my friends during all three of my pregnancies. They were a welcome source of laughter after exhausting days and were quick to swoop in with diapers when I ran out unexpectedly (accompanied by ice cream, of course). The dynamic between friends isn't as complicated as with family members, and this may make it easier for you to lean on your closest friends more than on family.

Caregivers will also form part of your support team as well as co-workers if you're lucky enough to work in an environment where personal bonds are possible. It doesn't matter who you make part of your care community as long as you trust them and they have you and your baby's best health in mind.

STAYING OPTIMISTIC

Postpartum depression is a reality. Hopefully, you won't experience it, but if you do, don't feel despondent. It happens to a lot of new mothers. There are ways you can make your postpartum life a little easier, but it all comes down to one thing: your attitude.

I'm not saying you can "think away" postpartum depression by staying positive, but it can help ease some of the symptoms. For one, taking a more balanced approach to motherhood will make a world of difference. Often, new mommies are so focused on doing everything right that they forget to stop and smell the roses—or in this case, the babies.

Here are some 'rules' you can apply to make your postpartum experience a more pleasant one.

Don't compare yourself: I know some new mothers look like they know the secret to keeping it together after giving birth. They are dressed fashionably all the time, have make-up on, perfect hair, and can somehow hold their baby in one arm, a week's worth of groceries in the other, and still manage to make it to the door gracefully. You're not a bad mother if you're not like them. Do things your way and to the best of your ability. I know that sounds cliché, but you are you. Comparing yourself to another mother will only breed unhappiness.

Don't compare babies: I know in this book, we cover a lot of milestones you can expect in the first six months of your baby's life, but I don't want you to get hung up on any of them. Each baby has their own time. It's easy for new moms to get sucked into the whirlpool of information, and they end up worrying about their child's development. You should try to find a balance; make sure your baby is on the right track but don't stress out if they weigh a little more/less or are a little slower at reaching milestones. It's not a competition.

Don't feel guilty: There will be times when you don't do things perfectly or as expected. Maybe your baby will go to bed tonight without having had a bath. You will probably feel guilty for letting that happen, but I want you to know that it is okay. Being a mom can awaken a strong guilt cycle, and you should do your best to catch yourself when it creeps closer. Tell yourself you are only human, just like all the other mothers who are doing their best to survive. As long as you love your kids and you're doing the best you can, then there is no reason to feel guilty about anything. Tomorrow is another chance to do better.

2

BABY CARE BASICS

*B*efore we jump into your baby's growth milestones for the first six months, I want to cover some of the fundamentals of caring for a newborn. This chapter targets the new mommies among the readers—those who are consumed by fear of the unknown when it comes to raising a little being. However, even if you're on your second or third pregnancy and anything like me, this chapter will be beneficial to you. Even after raising two kids, I still felt like I knew nothing when my third came along, so don't for a second feel inferior if you question your ability to mommy, even if it's not your first time around the crib.

DIAPERING

You'll be spending more time than you can imagine changing diapers—as many as ten times a day or more! In the beginning, you may think it is complicated, but the more you practice, the easier it will be to keep your little one clean and dry.

To change a diaper, you will need:

- Diaper
- Fasteners for cloth diapers
- Warm water and a washcloth or cotton balls. You can also use wet wipes, but keep in mind that your baby's skin is sensitive.
- Ointment or petroleum jelly to prevent diaper rash.
- Changing pad or towel to place under your baby.

You want your supplies all to be in reach. Don't leave your little one unattended, not even for a second.

After removing the soiled diaper, use a wet washcloth to wipe your baby clean.

Top tip: Always wipe from front to back, especially on girls, to avoid spreading bacteria that may cause urinary tract infections. I find it works well if you gently hold your baby by the ankles and lift them to clean underneath. Pay attention to cleaning in the creases of the thighs and buttocks.

If you have a boy, I suggest you get in the habit of placing a clean diaper over the penis. You don't want an unexpected shower!

Once you're done wiping, pat your baby dry and put on some baby bum cream.

When it comes to diapers, most people will choose disposable diapers for convenience. That being said, not everyone can afford to pay such high prices for disposable diapers, so cloth diapers it may have to be! Cloth diapers are way more affordable since you wash them, and they're more environmentally friendly.

If you're using cloth diapers, here are some tips to keep in mind:

- Use oversized pins with plastic safety heads. Always keep your hand between the pin and your baby's skin to ensure there aren't any pricking accidents.

- Empty soiled diapers into the toilet first before adding to the diaper pail. If you're worried about the odor, spray diapers with water and baking soda.
- Don't wash diapers with the rest of your laundry. As you know by now, your baby's skin is sensitive, and you will have to use a detergent that is hypoallergenic and specific for infants. Avoid using fabric softener or antistatic products you'd use on your clothes.
- Wash your hands thoroughly when you finish changing the diaper. You don't want any germs to spread.

Some tips for disposable diapers include:

- Empty the garbage at least once a day to prevent the growth of bacteria, not to mention the constant odor attack on your nose.
- Check for marks around your baby's legs and waist. If you find any, buy a looser fit next time or consider sizing up the diaper.

- If you see a rash form around your baby's legs and waist, it may be that your baby is sensitive to the specific brand of diaper. Change things up and see if it gets better.
- Don't place the waistline of the diaper on or above your little one's umbilical cord. That area should stay dry until the cord has fallen off, and any irritation should be avoided.
- For boys, always put the penis in a downward position before securing the diaper. This will stop any leaks.

If you see your baby has a diaper rash, don't panic. It's common for babies to get it from time to time. The problem comes when it happens often, lasts for two or more days, and gets progressively worse.

To prevent and help heal this painful complaint, keep the following in mind:

- Don't let your baby wear a wet and dirty diaper for long. Change their diaper as soon as you can.
- Be gentle when cleaning your baby. Hard rubbing will irritate your little one's skin

and may cause a rash. It will also definitely irritate an existing rash.

- Use ointment to prevent and heal any rashes. I suggest you buy one that contains zinc oxide as it acts as a barrier between your baby's skin and moisture.
- Choose a time of the day where you'll let your baby go diaper-free. Place your baby on a towel or cloth for any accidents, and if you have a boy, place a cloth diaper over the penis.

Before we move on, a quick word on your baby's umbilical stump. Your baby's stump should fall off after a week or two. When it does fall off, you will notice some blood or wetness; this is normal. But to make sure you're doing everything you can to get that pesky thing to fall off, you must:

- Keep the cord dry. The drier it is, the quicker it will fall off.
- Use warm water and soap to clean the cord only when it is visibly dirty. Pat dry gently afterward.
- Avoid giving your baby a tub bath while the stump is still attached.

- Call your baby's doctor if you smell something bad coming from the cord, the area around is red and inflamed, you can see yellow or green puss, it is bleeding, or if the cord stays soft and moist.

There you go, the basics of diapering. If you stick to these tips, you'll be a pro in no time!

BURPING

You'll soon notice that a good belch can take your baby from being a real grump-grump to their smiling, happy selves. Babies often get cranky while they're feeding or right after because the air they swallowed with the milk is causing discomfort. This is precisely why you should burp your baby during and after each feeding. I say during because sometimes the bubbles your little one swallowed are making them feel full before they're done eating. If you burp them during the feeding process, you'll be sure that their tummies are filled with nutritious milk and not just a lot of air.

To burp your baby, here are some tips I found work well:

- Use a burp cloth! I cannot stress this enough. You do not want to smell like sour milk the whole day.
- My first baby needed a gentle pat or rub to release all those air bubbles. The other two, however, needed a firmer hand. Start gently, but if you see nothing is happening, apply some more pressure. Bumping them up and down on your knee also works, but make sure not to go too wild, or they'll burp up their whole meal.
- Pat or rub on the left side of your baby's back. That is where their stomach is located.

There are three positions you can use to burp your baby: shoulder, face-down on your knee, or sitting. I suggest you give all of them a try to see what gets the job done.

On your shoulder: Hold your little one against your shoulder. Support their back with your one hand while you pat or rub their back with the other.

Face-down: Place your baby on their tummy across your lap. Hold them securely and pat or rub their back until they belch.

Sitting up: Let your baby sit in your lap while leaning forward into your one hand slightly. Use your other hand to rub or pat their back.

As your baby's head control improves, you can burp them while walking. Hold your baby with their back against your chest and apply some light pressure to their tummy. This will release all the trapped air bubbles.

If your baby doesn't burp, they may just not be a frequent burper. Some babies pass enough gas on their own so that you don't have to be too bothered.

RUB-A-DUB-DUB IN THE TUB

Bath time is usually a great time to bond with your newborn, and as they grow older, it may even become one of your and their favorite times of the day. That being said, it can also be a stressful time in the beginning. A million questions will be running through your mind when you get ready for your baby's first bath. When? How often? Is the water too hot or cold? Don't worry; here's everything you need to know to prepare you for bubbly fun.

Your Baby's First Bath

In the past, the nurses would whisk babies away right after birth to bathe them. This isn't the case anymore. The World Health Organization (2012) now recommends you wait 24 hours because there may be significant benefits in this delay. Your baby is very sensitive after being born, and when they're subjected to cold-induced stress, their body will have to work extra hard to keep itself warm, and this may cause blood sugar levels to drop. Furthermore, babies have a wax-like coating on their skin—called vernix—that retains heat but more importantly, acts as a barrier to infections.

So, your baby should only get a bath when at home, and even then, there is no set timetable. I was excited about bathing my three as soon as we got home, but I know of friends who decided to wait a week. They only wiped off any remaining blood and placenta from birth and made sure to clean the diaper area thoroughly every time. You can rub the vernix into your baby's skin to boost its antimicrobial properties and add moisture.

Babies do not need to have a bath often. Three times a week is more than enough since they don't really get dirty. However, if you plan to set up a bedtime routine for your baby, a nightly bath is fine as well. Remember that you should keep the umbilical stump dry at all times, so I don't recommend immersing your little one until the cord falls off completely.

How to Bathe Your Newborn

Let's start with you relaxing. Your baby's first bath can be a stress-free experience if you stop worrying so much. Yes, your baby is tiny and looks breakable; your little one may cry and look unhappy, but this doesn't mean you're doing anything wrong. I suggest you have a look at a nurse giving a newborn a bath—you won't be mistaken to think they're washing the dishes! This will put your mind at ease and make you realize that you won't break your baby.

Here's a step-by-step guide to giving your newborn a gentle sponge bath:

1. **Gather supplies.** Make sure everything you'll need is in reach. You'll need a washcloth and baby-safe soap, a dry towel, and a clean diaper. Never leave your little one unattended.

2. **Pick a spot.** The great thing about giving a newborn a bath is that you don't need to do it in a bathroom. Actually, the bathroom can be a chilly place and may leave your baby cold. You can use a baby bathtub, but that is not a necessity. As long as you and your baby are comfortable and warm, it doesn't matter where you decide to bathe them.

3. **Wash slowly.** Whether you place your baby in the baby bathtub or on a dry towel, cover your baby with an extra towel. You don't want them to get cold. Lift a small section at a time to wash and pat dry. Pay

special attention to any creases and rolls
and the diaper area.

As soon as the umbilical cord stump falls off, the fun
starts! Yes, it will be tricky at first, but it can be seen
as family bonding time when you ask your partner or
your baby's older sibling to help. Extra hands will
come in handy! Get your supplies and helpers, and
let's give your baby their first full bath.

1. **Fill the bath with two to three
   inches of water.** Keep the temperature
   between 90 and 100 degrees Fahrenheit. I
   know you may worry that the water is too
   hot; keep in mind that babies get cold easily,
   so don't make it too cold either. Use your
   wrist to test the water, or if you're too
   nervous, get yourself a thermometer.

2. **Support your baby's head.** Lower
   your little one into the tub while all the
   time keeping your hand behind their
   neck/head. Use a washcloth and baby
   soap to clean their tiny bodies. I
   recommend having more than one
   washcloth so that you can switch them out

as they get cold. Pay attention to creases, behind the ears, the neck, and genital areas.

3. **Don't use lotions and powders.** You may notice that your baby's skin looks dry. Don't give in to the temptation to slather on lotion—your baby's skin has natural oils. You can use coconut oil or petroleum jelly on dry patches on the ankles or wrists where dryness will cause discomfort due to the movement. Furthermore, although baby powder may seem like a nice touch, the particles may cause some respiratory problems when they get into your baby's lungs.

There are a lot of small things to think of when you give your baby their first bath, but don't worry, it will become second nature before you know it. One day, you'll blink, and your little one will be sitting up on their own and playing with toys in the tub.

Some of my most precious moments are when I would take a bath with my babies. There's nothing quite like feeling their soft skin against yours while relaxing in a nice bath. It's also the perfect time to entertain them with some bubbles!

EARS, NOSE, AND NAILS

You will need to pay special attention to your little one's ears, nose, and nails. Just as with bathing your baby, I know the idea of cleaning these areas is somewhat daunting. After all, we've established that, as mommies, we believe our babies are made from porcelain! But you have to change that mindset if you want your baby to grow up healthy. Treating your newborn like they're fragile is a good thing in some instances but not when it comes to cleanliness.

Ears

You have to be careful when you clean your baby's ears to avoid potentially damaging their hearing. For this reason, put away the cotton swabs! You won't be sticking anything inside your little one's ear. The only things you'll need are a washcloth or a cotton ball and warm water to clean the ear. This is easily done when you're giving your baby a bath.

Don't remove any earwax you see. It is healthy and protects and lubricates the ear canal. If the wax buildup is severe, ask your baby's doctor for advice. They will probably prescribe some ear drops to remove wax buildup.

To use ear drops, follow these steps:

1. Put your baby on their side.
2. Pull the lower earlobe back and down to open the canal.
3. Add the prescribed number of drops.
4. To ensure the drops don't run out of your baby's ear, keep them on their side for 10 minutes or so. You can then turn them onto their other side and let the excess drops run out onto a tissue.

If you see your baby tug at their ears regularly or if you see a yellow-green discharge, you should phone the pediatrician. It may be that a blocked ear canal is preventing your baby from hearing you, and the doctor will have to remove any wax that is interfering with hearing or causing discomfort.

Nose

This is one of my favorite features on a baby's face— the teeny-tiny little nose. But a blocked nose can cause a parent to go from peaceful to panic-mode in a split second. It is, unfortunately, part of the territory and will make even the most experienced parent worry.

Luckily, there are things you can do to make it easier for your baby to breathe easily again when their nose becomes stuffy.

Nose drops and suction bulb: Help loosen the sticky stuff by adding one or two drops of saline to your baby's nose. Afterward, use a rubber suction bulb to pull out the mucus. It's straightforward; squeeze the bulb before inserting it into a nostril, then slowly release, and it will suck out anything that is making your baby's breathing difficult. I recommended clearing your baby's nose before every feeding to help them breathe easily while eating.

Humidity: If there is moisture in the air, the mucus inside your baby's nose won't dry up so quickly and will be effortless to remove. Place a humidifier in your baby's room close to their crib but out of reach. If you don't have a humidifier and you're desperate, run a warm shower, close the bathroom door, and let them breathe the warm air.

Nails

I'm going to be honest, this is scary, but those itty-bitty nails will need a trim one time or another. Your baby may need a manicure in the first week after birth already and then every two or three days during the first two to three weeks. Their nails will need to harden before they stop growing so fast. And although their nails may feel soft, they can quickly turn into sharp weapons that cause scratches all over.

My mother suggested I peel or nibble off my baby's nails, and she's not the only one! That's the way a lot of old-school mommies did it, and we're still alive, right? Well, it may not be the best idea since you can accidentally peel off too much nail or transfer germs to your little one when you chew on their nails. Instead, get yourself scissors specifically made for the job. Baby scissors have rounded tips to prevent any poking accidents.

When trimming nails, press the fingertip away from the nail and follow the fingernail's natural curve as you cut. Remember to cut straight across when you're working on their tiny toes. And, here's the thing, you most likely will draw blood! Don't feel too sorry for yourself or your little one; just apply some pressure with a lint-free cloth to help the bleeding stop.

PENIS CARE

Things are a little more complicated when you have a boy. Firstly, you will have to decide if your son will be circumcised or not. This procedure will be done in the hospital, two or three days after birth, but it can also be performed later on. Once done, your doctor will advise you if you should change the dressing until the penis is healed entirely or leave it off altogether. The jury is out when it comes to which method is best, so it depends on you and the doctor.

After the penis is healed, no additional care is needed unless a small piece of foreskin remains behind. In that case, you'll want to pull back the skin every time you bathe your baby boy. The same goes for an uncircumcised penis. Make sure the foreskin does not stay stuck to the glans or head of the penis by pulling it down gently. You mustn't force this process, or you may cause a tear that will be very painful. Also, make sure to clean around the grooves of the penis head.

LAB TESTS

In the United States, each newborn will get screened for health disorders that aren't found at birth. Your doctor will do a blood test to check for genetic metabolic and hormone-related conditions, which may impact your baby's health at a later stage. This screening gives doctors the ability to diagnose and start treatment as soon as possible.

There are national screening recommendations, but ultimately, it depends on the state you live in. Here is what newborn screening may include.

Metabolic disorders like phenylketonuria, methylmalonic acidemia, tyrosinemia, maple syrup urine disease, citrullinemia, and medium-chain acyl CoA dehydrogenase deficiency. That's a mouthful, I know, but it's good to know if anything is wrong in this area since your baby's metabolism plays an important role in how their body functions.

Hormonal problems like congenital hypothyroidism and congenital adrenal hyperplasia.

Hemoglobin problems like sickle cell disease, hemoglobin SC disease, and beta thalassemia. Since hemoglobin carries oxygen around, this type of screening is vital to ensure your baby's health.

Other serious medical problems screened for include galactosemia, biotinidase deficiency, cystic fibrosis, Pompe disease, mucopolysaccharidosis type 1, spinal muscle atrophy, and x-linked adrenoleukodystrophy. Some states also screen for hearing loss and congenital heart disease.

I know you just read a lot of big words that sound frightening. And yes, while there are a lot of things that can be wrong, it doesn't mean they will be! But it's always better to be safe than sorry. After the newborn screening, you'll only have to wait four to seven days for the results. In this case, no news is good news as most labs only phone if your baby's tests were abnormal. Furthermore, if your little one does test positive, keep in mind that it doesn't mean your child has the condition. Doctors will order more tests to double-check.

IMMUNIZATIONS

If you want to protect your baby against life-threatening diseases, vaccination is a must. It is by far the safest and most effective preventive measures. Immunization is done at specific ages, and some vaccines will need to be given in spaced doses. In many cases, your child will have had to be vaccinated before starting school.

Here is a list of the immunizations of your baby's life starting from birth to 15 months old (CDC, 2020).

Vaccine	Birth	Month 1	Month 2	Month 4	Month 6	Month 9	Month 12	Month 15
Hepatitis B	1st dose	2nd dose			3rd dose			
Rotavirus		1st dose		2nd dose	3rd dose			
Diphtheria, tetanus, acellular pertussis			1st dose	2nd dose	3rd dose			4th dose
Haemophilus influenzae type B			1st dose	2nd dose			3rd dose	
Pneumococcal			1st dose	2nd dose	3rd dose		4th dose	
Polio			1st dose	2nd dose	3rd dose			

COMMON ILLNESSES

Babies do get ill, and even if they only get the common cold, I know as a parent, you'll be just as sick—with worry.

Here are some of the most common illnesses your little one may get during their young life.

Common cold: You can expect the sniffles, a sore throat, and mild fever to strike your baby up to five times a year! To help your baby get over the common cold, you can give them children's ibuprofen or acetaminophen to help break their fever. You can use saline drops or spray to keep their nasal passageways nice and moist and to prevent mucus from drying. It's during this time where a humidifier will also come in handy.

Respiratory syncytial virus: Kiddies under two are the most susceptible to this virus that affects the lungs. The symptoms usually mirror that of a cold, but if your child has a compromised immune system or any diseases, it can become serious quickly. If your child is wheezing, breathing too fast, struggling to take in any air, doesn't want to drink, and appears very tired, call your pediatrician immediately. Also, keep an eye out for a bluish tinge around their lips.

Roseola: You may not even realize that your child has Roseola since their symptoms may be minor. However, some kids get a high fever and suffer from congestion, coughing, and a patchy rash. This usually clears up in a week, but if your child's fever spikes or lasts longer than three days, you should contact your pediatrician.

Gastroenteritis: This isn't your average tummy ache! Also known as a stomach bug, gastroenteritis causes vomiting, diarrhea, and stomach pain. Various viruses can cause gastro; norovirus is one of the common ones and is often found in childcare centers. When your little one gets gastro, you will have to make sure they drink enough to make up for the fluids they lose from the runny tummy and possible vomiting. That being said, don't give too much liquid at once because your baby may not be able to hold it down.

Hand-foot-mouth disease: If your baby has painful-looking sores in their mouth and throat, it is most likely the Coxsackievirus. It usually shows up during summer and fall and is highly contagious; it spreads through touch, coughs, sneezes, and fecal matter. In addition to the sores in their mouth and throat, you may also see red blisters on their hands and the soles of their feet for up to 10 days. Children's ibuprofen or acetaminophen is the best way to ease the aches and pains, and to help with their sore throat, cold fluid and ice pops work wonders.

Pinkeye: This is one disease that can spread like wildfire through your household! Identified by an inflammation of the eye, a yellowish discharge, blurry vision, and crusty eyes, it is caused by a bacterial infection. To avoid your whole family getting pinkeye, everyone should keep their hands clean and stop sharing hand towels, blankets, and pillows.

Pinworms: When you see your child scratch their bottom, they may have tiny parasites annoying them. Babies and children usually get infected when they come into contact with another child or a surface contaminated with these parasites. If they then put their hands in their mouth, the eggs will land up in their digestive system, where they will hatch and lay eggs around your baby's anus. Doctors usually give a tape to put on the area at night to catch any worms and eggs for identification.

Most illnesses come and go without much fanfare, but some symptoms should raise a red flag and warrant a call to the doctor.

Dehydration: Sunken eyes, lethargy, and sticky mouth are signs that your baby is dehydrated. Keep an eye on how much they urinate. Fewer than three or four times a day and something is wrong.

High fever: If your baby is younger than six months and has a fever of 101 degrees Fahrenheit, then you should call a doctor.

Difficulty breathing: Wheezing, fast or challenging breathing, as well as long pauses between each breath are signs of concern.

Loss of appetite: Sick children won't show much interest in food, but when you see your baby's food and drink consumption is less than half what they'd normally eat and this lasts for two or more days, phone your doctor.

Before we move on to the chapter about breastfeeding, I want to add a section about picking up and carrying your baby—something which you'll be doing numerous times a day. And the bigger they get, the more challenging it will be to move them around without hurting yourself. So, let's have a look not at ergonomics in general, but a little thing I like to call baby-gonomics.

LIFTING AND CARRYING YOUR BABY

Let's face it, your baby will spend a lot of time in your arms, and there's nothing like cuddling such a sweet-smelling, soft little human. But you'll also have to transfer your little one from your arms to the changing table, bath, cot, and so on. This, too, will put a lot of strain on your body. Luckily for us, there are some ergonomic techniques to prevent any new-parent injuries.

1. Mind Your Posture

If you haven't done this already, you've undoubtedly seen it: lean to one side, pelvis forward, bouncing baby on one hip. This is the typical "parent pose," which you need to learn to undo. It's uncomfortable and will do a number on your back. To avoid any pains and strains, hold your baby with both arms while keeping your pelvis centered. Support your baby under their bum and if they still need neck support, use your other hand to press them close to you. When you have to use the classic hip carry, remember to switch sides often to balance things out and go back to a balanced posture as soon as you can.

The secret is to keep your little one's weight as close to your center of gravity as possible. This will reduce any side, back, or front pulling—your lumbar paraspinal and QL muscles will thank you!

2. Change Position

If you always carry your little one the same way, you will surely put unnecessary strain on specific muscles day after day. Switch things up by using baby carriers or changing the position you're holding your baby in regularly. Focus on your shoulders, neck, chest, and arms and feel if there are any aches and pains. If a specific area feels very sore, try to use a carrying posture that doesn't put too much pressure on it.

3. Bend at the Hip

Picking up and putting down your little one so many times a day will put a strain on your lower back if done incorrectly. Keep some points in mind when you have to bend to move your baby around:

- Hug your little one close to your chest.
- Spread your feet a few inches wider than shoulder-width apart.
- Bend your knees a little. When picking the baby up from the floor, use your legs and glutes to lift from a squatting position. Keep your back straight and neck long. Don't curl your back and try to use it to do all the work.
- Hinge your hips back. If you tuck your tailbone down a fraction, you'll activate your abdominal muscles, and this will protect your back.
- Set your baby down. This technique can also be used when you pick your baby up.

You're one of the most important people in your little one's life, and that is why you should take care not to hurt yourself. Also, you don't want to tear a muscle, lose your footing, and fall with your baby in your arms!

∼

3

BREASTFEEDING

*I*nstead of drinking milk the first time they nurse, your baby will be drinking colostrum. This yellowish liquid is rich in antibodies that will boost their immune system. It will take a few days for your real milk to come in. But don't worry, you will know when it arrives. For one, your breasts will feel as if they're about to burst. Luckily, your baby will be able to help you get rid of this engorgement, and the more you nurse, the better your breasts will feel.

I know the main concern you will have as a new mom is whether your baby is eating enough since it is difficult to tell. When your little one nurses straight from the breast, you won't be able to count the ounces but will have to rely on other signs that show they're feeding enough. The first thing to look for is if you can see and hear your baby swallowing. Second, if you find yourself feeling as if you're changing their diaper every few minutes (I know it feels like that even though it isn't the case), then your baby is eating enough. The ideal is changing eight to ten diapers filled with urine and yellow, soft stools.

However, if your baby exhibits the below signs, give the doctor a call:

- Your little one feeds for 10 minutes or less.
- Your baby is lethargic or overly fussy frequently.
- Your baby's skin has a yellow tinge.
- Your baby's stools are dark and hard.

Breastfeeding has a lot of benefits. Breast milk contains all the nutrients your baby needs, and it is easier to digest than formula. Furthermore, it has antibodies, which will boost your baby's immune system. Although it is a natural process, it doesn't come naturally to everyone, and some mommies may find it challenging. But considering all the positive things that come from breastfeeding, you should try your best to prepare yourself for this crucial new job you'll have.

With patience, a little effort, and support, both you and your baby will get the hang of it. Remember that your baby hasn't nursed yet, so you're both newbies at this. Trust your body, and you'll be fine.

GETTING STARTED

Start breastfeeding in the hospital with the help of a nurse or a lactation consultant. Your newborn will know how to suck, but you will need their lips to latch around your nipple. This will take some trial and error, and having someone help you will ensure that you don't get discouraged.

Getting your baby to latch may prove difficult at times; they may not know what to do when they come face to face with your breast, and as soon as they figure it out and start suckling, your nipple may slip out of their mouth, causing a lot of unhappiness. You may not get it right for a whole day, but that doesn't mean your baby will starve. Babies are born with extra energy stores to make up for any difficulties feeding.

I remember it was an uphill battle with baby number one. I was so frustrated after trying for hours, and feeling like my baby was starving due to my inexperience didn't help the situation. The relief I felt after my little one latched for the first time was overwhelming. I think we both gave a sigh of relief after that!

To get your baby to latch, you can try the following:

1. Turn your baby on their side so that they're facing you with your bellies touching. Prop them up with a pillow if you find it more comfortable, and proceed to hold your little one up to your breast. Don't lean toward your baby; instead, bring them to meet your breast.

2. Put your thumb and fingers around the areola. Tilt your baby's head back and rub

your nipple against their lips until they open their mouth.

3. To help your baby scoop up your breast, place their lower jaw well below the nipple and tilt the head forward. Your baby will most likely take the entire nipple and 1 ½ inches of your areola into their mouth.

HOW TO HOLD YOUR NURSING BABY

There's not a hard and fast way to hold your baby during feeding time. It comes down to what is comfortable for you and your little one. You can even use a breastfeeding pillow if you feel like it.

Here are the three most common ways to cradle your baby.

Cradle hold: Baby lays lengthwise across your tummy while you use one hand to support their head and the other their bottom.

Football hold: Put your baby beside you lengthwise and with their face up. Lay them along the length of your arm and guide their head to your breast. This is a very comfortable position if you've had a C-section.

Lying down: Lie on your right side and put your baby on their left side facing your chest. Make sure their mouth is at the same height as your nipple. Use your free hand to guide your baby's mouth toward the nipple on your right (closest to the bed).

HOW OFTEN TO BREASTFEED

Babies are simple creatures. They sleep, eat, poop, and urinate. This is why it is usually fairly straight-forward to figure out what exactly your baby is crying about. If you can set up an eating schedule, you'll be able to tell the difference between an "I am wet" cry and a "Please feed me" cry.

After your baby eats, you should offer your breast again in two hours. In the beginning, your little one may not get much milk, but as soon as your supply kicks in, your baby will be happy. The first nursing sessions may be short since your baby is still figuring out how to latch, suck, and swallow. But as soon as they get the hang of it, you're looking at feedings that are between 20 and 40 minutes long—on each breast!

11 THINGS TO KNOW ABOUT
BREASTFEEDING

1. It may not be everything you expected.

The first days of breastfeeding are not going to feel magical; it will be a learning curve for you and your little one. You are both doing something you've never done before, and it may be overwhelming. But don't worry, it gets better!

2. You'll learn quickly.

It will only be a few days before you and your baby know precisely what to do during feedings. Your little one will know how to latch, and your nipples won't be as sensitive since they will be used to being sucked on frequently. When you're over the trial and error phase, you can start to enjoy the bonding experience thoroughly.

3. Cramping happens.

Menstrual-like cramps are common while breastfeeding. The hormone oxytocin is to blame—it's not called the bonding hormone for nothing. This hormone will help your uterus go back to its pre-pregnancy shape and size, so don't curse it too much.

4. It's not just working moms who pump milk.

A breast pump is such a great invention. I like it for the simple fact that you can monitor how much your baby is drinking. It also gives you back some of your independence because you can be away from your baby for a while since they'll have food on hand.

5. It's okay to feel as if breastfeeding is all you do.

The first few months of your baby's life may end up being a blur considering that the main thing you'll remember is the constant feedings. Young babies do need to eat a lot, but instead of looking at the negative side of breastfeeding, consider that this is a bonding experience between you and your little angel.

6. You'll be extra hungry and thirsty.

It takes a lot out of a mommy when their baby feeds, so you'll burn a lot of calories and get dehydrated quickly. In fact, your body can burn up to 500 calories a day producing milk. No wonder you'll want to eat and drink more than usual.

7. You don't have to limit your diet so much.

You were pregnant for nine months, and during this time, you had to avoid a lot of foods. Now that you're breastfeeding, you can lift most of the restrictions. You should still aim to follow a healthy diet because your baby will essentially be eating what you eat. Keep an eye out for any food allergies or irritation. My little girl got the worst gas whenever I ate white bread.

8. Make it a team effort.

Your partner can help when it comes to nursing. If you pump, they can take nightly feedings so that you can get some much-needed rest. Or maybe put them on burping after each nursing session. Involve your partner in this beautiful process, even if it is just asking for a glass of water while you're breastfeeding.

9. Don't look for symmetry.

One breast may produce more milk than the other, and there is nothing wrong with that. If your baby is drinking enough and you're not experiencing any discomfort (other than the obvious), there's no reason why you should try and change it.

10. Don't feel guilty.

If you can't continue breastfeeding your baby and have to switch over to formula, don't let any guilt get to you. It is okay to stop.

11. Keep going.

A lot of people think it is taboo to continue breast-feeding beyond a year. But that doesn't mean you should listen to them. I think listening to your baby is a much better plan. If your little one wants to continue breastfeeding, don't stop. There is nothing wrong with nursing your little one for however long they—and you—want to continue.

4

MONTH ONE

One thing is sure, the first few weeks with your newborn in your arms are going to be mostly a magical time. But you will also go through a hard time as you learn to feed your little one, put them to sleep, and try to figure out what each cry or coo means. Your baby will keep you on your feet, even when you're trying to sleep.

I don't want you to worry about the difficult times of the day. Tomorrow you'll face different challenges and yesterday's will be a thing of the past. Babies go through a lot of changes as they grow, but to them, life couldn't be simpler. The only things that matter to them are having a full tummy, a safe and comfortable place to sleep, a clean diaper, and cuddles and love. It is the parents who usually complicate things, mainly due to worrying about everything.

Of course, your life will feel considerably more complex. The best advice I can give you during your transition into motherhood is to focus on your baby's essential needs only. You shouldn't overwhelm yourself with thoughts about the future too much at this time. Enjoy the new human being in your life; forget about checking your email, ease up on your household chores, and order dinner or ask your partner to cook.

YOUR BABY'S REFLEXES

When your baby enters the world, they will have a set of reflexes meant to protect them and make sure they get the care they need. It may take a while for your parenting instincts to kick in, so nature made sure your baby would survive during this time.

Some of these early reflexes include:

Rooting reflex: The rooting reflex helps babies locate the breast or bottle. It gets triggered as soon as your baby's mouth touches the nipple or teat. You can also prompt this reflex by gently stroking the corner of your baby's mouth in the direction of the nipple. Your little one will instinctively turn their head in that direction to 'root.'

Sucking reflex: This is probably the most important reflex newborns have. It happens right after the rooting reflex and allows your baby to suck and swallow milk.

Palmar reflex: When your baby grabs your finger when you put it in their palm.

Moro reflex: The sudden jump when your baby gets startled.

Keep an eye out for the above, but remember that all babies are different, so you shouldn't worry if your little one doesn't have one of these early reflexes. Your baby's doctor will check all the reflexes to make sure they are okay.

NEWBORN SENSES

Your baby's senses kick in the moment they're born. They may not work at an optimal level yet, but they're developing more every second of the day.

Vision: Your newborn's eyes will be puffy and swollen from delivery, but they're still able to see mommy's face and close-up objects. Nurses will administer a protective antibiotic eye cream right after birth, and this will make your baby's vision a little blurry for a while. You may also see that your baby's eyes may cross at times. That is nothing to be concerned about. The eye muscles aren't fully developed yet, so controlling eye movement is a little challenging.

Hearing: Your baby will already know the sound of your voice; they heard it in the womb. So, although their hearing isn't fully developed, they'll recognize when mommy is talking, which will calm them.

Taste: Newborn babies have a highly developed sense of taste, and they will be able to tell the difference between sweet and bitter. As you can imagine, they prefer sweet over bitter, which is great considering that breast milk and formula fit the bill.

Smell: Your baby will recognize your scent as soon as they are placed in your arms.

Touch: This is the most developed sense at birth and the reason why cuddling is so rewarding for your baby. They will want to feel the softness of your face and will delight in gentle strokes on their body.

YOUR BABY'S HEALTH

The first month will most probably be nerve-wracking when it comes to worrying about your baby's health. Here are some issues that may cause you sleepless nights, even though a lot of them aren't serious.

Curled-up body: Your baby lived in a tiny space for a long time and then had to be pushed through a narrow birth canal. It is to be expected that their body will look somewhat scrunched up for some time. Your little one's hands will be tiny fists, and their arms and legs will be tucked close to their body. They will stay in this fetal position for a while, but their muscles will slowly start to relax over time.

Swollen sex organs: This is temporary and is caused by your hormones still circulating in your baby's body. The swelling will go down with time. These hormones are also responsible for a milky discharge from their nipples, as well as a vaginal discharge, which will also go away in a week or two.

Weight loss: Newborn babies can drop up to 10% of their weight after birth. This is due to post-delivery fluid loss. You should only be concerned if their weight continues to drop five days after birth. You will see that your little one will pick up and even surpass their birth weight at the two-week post-birth mark.

Crying: Newborns cry—a lot. That is the only way they can communicate. You will get used to all the different types of whimpers and wails in no time. A crying baby, believe it or not, is a healthy one, so when your baby isn't crying a lot—even when you know they are hungry or soiled their diaper—you should contact the doctor. Excessive crying may make you wonder if your baby has colic. But keep in mind that colic symptoms include balled-up fists, closed or wide-open knees pulled to their chest, flailing limbs, too much gas, and holding their breath for short bouts. There is a rule of three when it comes to diagnosing colic: three hours of crying, three days a week, and for three weeks.

MONTH ONE MILESTONES

A lot is happening with your little one after birth. There's a lot of growth and development going on behind the scenes.

You can expect to see some growth spurts at the following ages:

- 7-10 days
- 2-3 weeks
- 4-6 weeks
- 3 months

During these times, it may feel like your baby is constantly nursing. And when they're not feeding, they're sleeping. This is perfectly normal as your baby needs extra nourishment and rest during these growth spurts.

When it comes to developmental milestones, you can expect to see your baby:

- Lift their head briefly during tummy time.
- Focus on your face.
- Bring their hands to your face.
- Suckle better.

Some babies will be able to respond to loud noise in one way or another, use vocalizations other than crying, and smile when you smile.

BABY FEEDING SCHEDULE

Even with all the differences between each baby, one thing is sure, breastfed babies will need to eat more than bottle-fed ones. The reason behind this is that breast milk digests easier than formula. It is recommended that your baby nurse for the first time within one hour of birth. No rest for the weary, right? But it doesn't end there; your little one will need eight to twelve feedings daily for the first few weeks of their life.

Your baby should not go for more than four hours without feeding. There will be times when you have to disturb that sweet little face while they're sleeping for their next feeding. You want them to gain the right amount of weight, and to do that, they need to get in enough calories.

The feeding pattern will get a little more predictable as your baby grows and they can take in more milk at one feeding.

When it comes to bottle-fed babies, the same rule applies: They should eat on demand every two to three hours.

Some rules apply to both breastfed and bottle babies:

- Don't give your baby liquids other than breast milk or formula for the first year of their life. Other fluids don't contain the right nutrients and will most likely upset your baby's tummy. You can, however, introduce water at the six-month mark.
- Don't add any cereal or other chunks to the bottle. Your baby's digestive system is not mature enough yet to handle cereal. Furthermore, it can be a choking hazard.

- Don't add honey to your baby's milk. It can be dangerous and cause what is known as infant botulism (Fletcher, 2019).

Sticking to a Schedule

You'll fall in love with schedules when you're a parent. Anything from eating, sleeping, and general activities can be scheduled. When it comes to feeding, your child will naturally fall into a pattern. Their tummy just needs to grow, and you need to produce enough milk to fill them up in one sitting. This usually happens between two and four months.

But let's first look at your little one's hunger cues:

- Your baby grabs and feels around your chest as they look for a nipple.
- Their fist is in their mouth.
- You can hear them smack their lips. Licking is also a good indication of hunger.
- Your little one is irritable and fussy. It's never a good idea to let your baby enter the 'hangry' (hungry and angry) zone—don't wait too long to feed them.

When it comes to introducing a sleep/feed schedule, you will have to wait until your baby is a few months old. For example, when your tiny tot is four months old and wakes up every five hours, make sure to adjust the feeding time to fit in with your schedule. If you feed them at 9 pm, they'll wake up at 2 am for their next meal. This cuts into your much-needed nighttime winks. Instead, feed your baby at 11 pm, and you'll only have to get up at 4 am for the next round of nursing.

My Baby Is Still Hungry

Remember those growth spurts I mentioned earlier? Well, during these times, your baby will eat more frequently. So, if your baby still seems hungry, give them more food. It isn't possible to overfeed a baby who drinks breast milk exclusively, but you can give bottle-fed babies too much food. This is why you must get to know your baby's hunger cues to make sure they're hungry and not just looking for the bottle as comfort.

You may also have a baby who "cluster feeds." This means they will drink more during specific times than others. If you're lucky, your little one will cluster feed in the later afternoon or early evening, which means they will sleep longer at night. Yay for small mercies! Cluster feeding is, however, more common in breastfed babies.

INFANT SLEEP NEEDS

Newborns will sleep most of the time, but you will notice that it comes in short segments. As your baby gets older, the amount they sleep will decrease slowly, but the time they sleep during the night will increase. Thank goodness!

In general, you can expect newborns to sleep eight to nine hours during the day and about eight at night. But as mentioned above, it may only be in increments of one to two hours at a time. It will only be at the three-month mark that your little one will sleep through the night.

There may be instances where your baby struggles to sleep through the night due to separation anxiety. When your little one is still small, they don't understand that the separation is only temporary, and they will become upset.

Another vital part of putting your baby to sleep is the ability to recognize signs of sleep readiness. If you can see when your baby is sleepy, you can teach them to fall asleep on their own and only be there to comfort them when they wake up.

Signs that your baby is looking to get some shut-eye include:

- Rubbing eyes
- Yawning
- Turning their head away from you
- Fussing

I will cover various sleep training methods further on in this book. It may be something you want to consider as it fits in nicely with scheduling feedings also.

YOUR BABY'S FIRST PUBLIC APPEARANCE

I know you may be asking yourself when is it safe to introduce your baby to the outside world. Your baby is beautiful, so of course, you want everyone in the park to ooh and aah at them. Then again, it's also a worrisome topic, especially for first-time parents.

Infants don't have strong immune systems yet and won't be able to fight off sickness. But according to pediatric experts, you can take your newborn out in public right away if you follow some safety precautions. The sunlight and fresh air will be good for you and your baby, but keep the following in mind when you take your little one for an outing.

Too much sun is a bad thing: Although the sun provides vitamin D—something your baby can never have too much of—sunburn is a reality. Your baby's skin is still thin and soft and will easily get burnt. For this reason, limit direct sun exposure to 15 minutes and always use sunscreen.

Watch out for germy hands: What do people do when they see a baby? They go in for the cheeks! They don't give a second thought to the germs on their hands. It's smart to ask strangers and other children to look but not touch. When it comes to family members, don't feel that you have to allow them to hold your baby. If you notice that your family member has a runny nose and still tries to touch your baby, you have the right to say no politely.

Choose the location wisely: Stay away from germ central station—schools, hospitals, doctors' offices, daycare centers, airplanes, etc. When you do have to go to these places, keep your baby as close to you as possible or cover them in the carrier or stroller. Also, make sure to wash your hands frequently. You don't want to pass along something you picked up from dirty surfaces or shaking hands.

Keep the weather in mind: Dress your baby appropriately. New parents often fall into the trap of believing that babies need to be dressed extra warm. This isn't the case, and your baby may overheat if overdressed. If you're not sure, look at how you are dressed and then put the same amount of clothes on your baby. You can always take a blanket just in case.

If you were to see the baby bag I always took with me when I went out, you'd laugh. I was prepared for rain, sunshine, or if you ask my husband, the apocalypse! You may not want to go as far as I did, but it is better to have everything you need on hand for your baby's comfort and well-being.

5

MONTH TWO

*N*ow that we have managed the first month of your baby's presence in your new daily routine, I am sure the initial concerns and uncharted territory feel a bit more familiar, correct? Of course, you are only starting on the exciting path, but as we go through the motions of the following weeks' progress, everything will start feeling more natural.

Naturally, there will be changes. We see new developments as the weeks pass, but all of this is usually positive and interesting, believe me! If you feel that you need to do some more research on what is coming, a good mom-friend is always great to confide in or ask for extra advice. After all, experience is a strong validator and teacher, so always feel free to approach someone you trust for that little bit of wisdom over a few minutes of tea.

Let us have a look at what is to be expected in the next four weeks of your tiny tot's development and cover some of the most important aspects of the journey through the second month. You will notice small changes compared to the first month of your baby's life, so here are a few exciting things you can look forward to!

YOUR BABY'S DEVELOPMENT

Going through month two, you should start seeing more of your baby's personality and reactions to basic stimuli. Do not fret if your baby does not exhibit these traits as quickly as you had hoped because, like everyone, they are just going at their own pace. There is no rush to perform at peak levels; all babies are individuals. Treat this time as a relaxed way to examine the progress of their motor skills, senses, and communication. But don't worry about that last part too much! No one expects your baby to have a vocabulary, but you will notice little things they react to when you speak to them. However, I will cover that a little bit later in this chapter. For now, we will cover motor skills to make sure you know what is ideal.

Motor Skills

You will be able to see changes in motor skills in how your baby learns to control their body, for instance, the increase in steadying their movements. There is usually an increase in strength as well, where you will notice that it is easier for your baby to lift their head by themselves or coordinate hand-eye collaboration.

Many new moms ask why babies tend to suckle on their fingers, another sign of their baby's improved motor skills. This is not anything to be alarmed about —usually. Babies develop a stronger sucking ability, and normally sucking on two of three fingers is their way of comforting themselves.

You might notice those overly jerking motions in baby's limbs are slightly more fluid and controlled. While they might not yet be able to handle toys effectively, do not be surprised if your baby's eyes follow colorful items dangling in front of him or her.

In most cases, they might even reach out to a toy from a mobile at this stage, evidence that their coordination and discernment of objects are developing. This is also where their depth perception starts kicking in, and those cute reaches for moving objects are telling you that they are measuring distance. By this time, you will find it irresistible to play with them! After all, you're here to have fun with your baby as you learn to engage successfully in that bond.

Look at That! Senses Are Kicking In!

Apart from what you notice in your baby's interaction with objects, their eyes are still not fully developed, so you might still have to move closer for them to learn to recognize your face. Use feeding time, for instance, to allow this closeness to instill your image in your baby's visual capacity. You will detect their ability to follow moving objects as you walk past or even in less perceptible motions such as cocking your head or moving your arms. Constant exposure to mild, calm movement will teach your baby's eyes to adjust to you and other surroundings.

With their eyes learning to discern items in their environment, your baby's hearing should also display improvement. At this stage, their ears acquire a sensitivity to noise levels and might respond to sounds by looking in the direction of a sound, or they may even appear to get anxious when exposed to too much sound contamination. They will need less volume and more substance to acquire the balance.

Talk—a lot.

Make sure that you talk often to your baby, not only to encourage their hearing but also to form a unique sense of communication between parent and child. Although your baby will not yet understand your obvious wisdom, you want them to get to know mommy and daddy's voices. Mind the tone of your voice to establish specific intonations and emotion that will help them learn what you sound like.

Since we are on the subject of communication, remember that this is not a specified avenue. In the second month, babies are more likely to let you know what they feel by crying, sometimes gurgling or moaning. Some moms have even managed to get this down to a science and can tell what kind of cry identifies the problem. These moms can tell by a single crying spell whether it is a wet bum, hungry tummy, or gas discomfort. This magic comes with experience, so do not feel bad if you fail to understand the mechanics of your baby's crying yet. It comes with the weeks that pass. Mostly, babies communicate in this most basic manner. Still, sometimes, you will be elated to see a smile that is not necessarily a manifestation of cramps, but indeed a true, toothless grin for mom and dad. This is one of the best parts, especially when your little one responds to your voice with a smile, acknowledging your affection.

Remember that the more you talk to your baby, the more likely they are to develop speech sooner and maybe form words in the following months. On that note, I believe a lot of new parents are unsure about how to speak to their babies. Trust me, it is not nearly as complicated as you think. The keyword is 'natural.' Always do what comes naturally, but when in doubt, here are some suggestions that work very well.

Chatting Up a Storm or Just Paying Attention

- Although babies need attention from both parents, there is proof that one-on-one chats help lessen any distractions so that they can focus more on what is being said.

- Baby talk is usually best when sounding like a song.
- Make sure that you look them in the eyes when having this personal talk time to establish a link of focus between you and your baby. With no distractions, they are more likely to pay attention to words and the affection of the conversation.
- Do not be surprised if your baby tries to talk back to you. This is adorable and should be encouraged, so do not interrupt it or look away from them when they talk. This might make them feel dismissed or wrong, so make a fuss about their efforts and watch the show! It matters greatly for them to know that you are listening, that you care.
- Not all speech is ideal. Television is not a substitute for personal language exchange or developing individuality, so try to avoid that as a medium for language advancement.
- Baby talk is a good start, but also mix it up with some general adult talk to establish some grounds for the correct pronunciation of words for good measure. It will also

benefit your baby's senses to be exposed to a variety of motivations.

HOW TO STIMULATE YOUR BABY'S SENSES

Stimulating your baby's senses is not all about movement and chatting, though. As much as that is a pivotal part of their development, make a note to actively stimulate your baby's senses in other ways such as baby massage (yes, it's a thing), tummy time, or playing together with one or both parents. The latter is always ideal, but it is difficult in this rush of daily life to get optimal playtime with both mom and dad.

Baby Massage

Baby massage is best when things are not frantic and you have some quality time to invest. Massage is best after baby's nap or after a bath because you and your baby need to be relaxed. Make sure the room temperature is warm and comfortable before you start. Don't stress about doing a professional job, okay? This is about bonding and calming your baby. Emotionally, your baby will learn to trust you and rely on these moments to feel safe.

Start with the soles of the feet and move up the legs with smooth strokes toward your baby's hips. Use cream or a tiny bit of massage oil to ease friction on the skin. This would be a great time to get rid of excess wind by resting the back of the baby's knee over your hand and gently bending the thigh toward the tummy. Move slowly and gently.

From the shoulders, massage down over your baby's chest and take turns to rub in long strokes from your baby's shoulders down to their wrists to work on the arms. Make sure that you wipe their hands clean for when they might suckle on their fingers. To massage your baby's tummy, avoid the navel if the cord has not healed completely yet. Take care not to apply pressure and circularly move your hand. Move clockwise, but if your baby starts displaying irritation or discomfort, cease your motions.

Now you can move to your baby's face, but make sure your nails are short. Use the pads of your fingers, stroking their forehead and along the sides of their face. This is usually a great time to play, being so close to your baby's face and having those soft cheeks between your fingers for a light tickle or giggle. Be careful when massaging the scalp and move in tight circles with your fingertips.

Gauge your baby's behavior and reaction to your touch. If they become fussy, it is a sign that they are tired or had their fill of the moment. However, if your baby seems relaxed and content, continue to massage the back by slowly turning the baby on their tummy and running your hands from their upper back down to their feet.

What on Earth Is Tummy Time?

Now, I know that tummy time sounds like something to do with food, but it is, in fact, an excellent way to promote upper body strength in your baby's shoulders, neck, and head. Strengthening these muscles is imperative to the effective development of your baby's ability to crawl or hold up their head.

Later, when your baby learns to walk, they will need to be strong enough to pull themselves up. Take up to five minutes every day to play with your baby while they lie on their tummy to make sure they learn to exert these muscles safely. You will soon notice that they quickly learn to lift their head or rear to peek over objects from this position. Well done, you! But don't forget to put your baby on their back before sleep.

Fun and Games

Playing together, as I stated before, is an excellent way to bond, but this is very important in manipulating your baby's mood and emotional advances. Playing with your baby instills a feeling of love, trust, and security in them, and you do not have to invest in fancy toys or gadgets at all. In fact, the more natural your interaction, the better. Talk to your baby, read from a book, or sing cheerful songs.

All this interaction will promote your baby's ability to form words, understand speech, and learn to duplicate your words and body language. Playing games creates an aptitude for identifying patterns, even at a young age, so feel free to play games like peekaboo. Smiling at your little one a lot—which won't be hard to do—will release positive chemicals in their brain and evoke a feeling of happiness, serenity, and safety. Since you are the one playing with them, they will no doubt develop a strong fondness for you.

FEEDING AND ITS FRENZIES

At the second month mark, feeding your baby may change due to activity or necessity, but there is no specific set of rules in this regard. You can always supplement or change to a formula feeding should you wish to.

What's the Formula?

Supplementing is when you add occasional feedings by bottle instead of only breastfeeding. This typically comes into play if it is more convenient for mom if she has to go back to work or due to circumstances like a decline in available breast milk. Premature babies and babies with some medical conditions need additional feeding other than just breast milk. If you are concerned about starting to supplement with the bottle for any reason, your physician can determine whether it is safe to do so.

An important footnote for moms who choose to introduce formula while using breastmilk: Do not mix your breastmilk with your unmixed formula powder. For safety reasons, it is best to use water as directed by the manufacturer.

Although most health organizations recommend exclusively breastfeeding up to the first six months (or even longer) while solid food is introduced, there are also concrete reasons for the alternative. It differs from mother to mother with varying lifestyles, so ultimately, that decision is entirely up to you.

Speak to your pediatrician to make sure you have the right advice before continuing with bottle-feeding. Most doctors will suggest formula with iron fortification, especially for the first year of a baby's life. Still, if your baby vomits, has diarrhea, develops a rash, cries excessively, or has a lot of gas after you start them on formula, they might be allergic. It would be wise to halt formula feeding immediately and see the doctor for other options. After all, your little one's health is the most important. On that note, though, that does not mean that your health is less significant because switching to formula also affects mom's body. Let me stress some suitable methods by which to make a smooth transition from breastfeeding for your body.

When you opt for supplementation, try to start slow with one or two bottles per day so that your breast milk production can adjust. You see, your breasts only produce as much milk as used every day, so as you add more formula feedings, your milk supply should decline proportionately.

Needless to say, if you suddenly just stop breastfeeding, your milk ducts might become blocked, or you might develop breast engorgement. This is when your milk supply is too high in relation to your delivery, and it builds up. Trust me, you do not want to have those hard, painful, lumpy, swollen breasts while having to take care of a small infant! Plus, you could get what is commonly known as milk fever on top of it. All that can be avoided if you gradually stop breastfeeding and allow your milk production to cease.

If you find that your breasts still produce too much milk, consider pumping. This will alleviate the thickness and discomfort of swollen breasts. Besides, you can store your breast milk should you find that your baby takes longer to get used to their formula.

You might find that formula affects your baby's digestive system differently as well, but this is usually par for the course. Some of the changes might take longer than others, but some will help you monitor the pace of the conversion.

Babies might not like the taste of the formula and reject bottle feedings, or they might simply prefer to get breast milk specifically from mom. Getting dad or someone else to bottle feed the baby might be a good idea to wean them from the feedings they get from mom. Waiting longer between feedings is very important. You see, your baby's digestive system makes quick work of breast milk while formula takes longer to digest, so they may feel too full for frequent feedings from the bottle.

Also, if your little one's poop is less frequent, it is just part of the change in their diet. You might notice that their bowel movements change in color or consistency, but this is because of the addition of the formula.

Sometimes, baby's diet changes will influence their moods or sleep patterns, just as changes in our diets and lives have an impact on our sleep. Many parents mistakenly think that baby's erratic sleep patterns will diminish as the weeks pass, but this is not a cut-and-dried matter at all, unfortunately. Many factors influence the sleeping habits of infants, so let us have a look at those and see what could help assess your baby's development based on their napping needs.

NAPPING AND CHANGING SLEEPING PATTERNS

Don't you just love the term "pajama drill"? In most parents, it evokes a feeling of dread and fatigue because we all know that sleep becomes a myth during those first few weeks with a newborn in the house. Much as we love our babies, the sporadic sleep schedule accompanying the first few weeks can be daunting. Many new parents mistakenly believe that their baby's sleep patterns automatically improve as the weeks progress, but this is not true for everyone.

New babies bring a lot of mystery with them, each being unique in their needs and innate attributes, which leaves most parents worrying about what the norm is. I bet you have been asking yourself how many hours your baby should be sleeping at this stage and if there is a specific time that is ideal for putting your infant to sleep. Let's have a look at the realistic expectations.

Initially, babies tend to sleep in short bursts because of their feeding needs. The latter is more frequent in the first four weeks, but as we enter the second month, your baby should realistically sleep between 14 and 18 hours. This sounds like a lot, but remember, this is the total amount of hours with feeding gaps in between. To optimize this, I suggest an early day start, probably around 7 am.

That way you can ensure that your baby's day closes at around about the same time as yours, making it easier to coordinate schedules. More detailed? Let me explain. Usually, a baby's naptime runs at one to two hours of napping and, equally, one to two hours of awake time. Easy to keep track of! The trick is to wake your baby for feeding if they sleep more than two hours at a time during the day. This way, you regulate a pattern of sleep/wake consistency, and your baby will not be too hungry at night or stay up longer than need be.

Speaking of nighttime sleep, an ideal time for night sleep is about 10 pm. It is normal for your baby to still doze on and off during the night, but at this stage of development, you should notice a longer stretch of snores per night at about four to eight hours. Once again, this is the ideal measure, but by no means is it written in stone, so do not feel alarmed if your baby's routine is slightly different.

Many mothers lament not knowing the subtle ways to help their babies fall asleep easier. I know I, for one, have spent hours trying to put my babies to sleep—only to fall asleep myself! An excellent way to lull babies to sleep is to use white noise at a low volume, swaddling, or moving around gently. Swaddling keeps your baby wrapped up tightly, preventing too much movement that might impair their ability to fall asleep, and it keeps the body tucked in and warm. When it comes to movement, you probably have heard stories, or maybe you were one of those babies who only fell asleep riding in a car. Motion is very soothing.

BRIGHT SMILES AND HAPPY FACES

You see it sometimes, but your family and friends probably tell you that your baby is smiling because of gas, cramps, or reflexes. This may be true for babies up to two months, but during a baby's second month, you can expect that smile to start meaning something! How can you tell? Easy.

Most babies show us their real smiles between one-and-a-half months to three months of age. The difference between reflex and a genuine smile is the timing of the smile and how long it lasts.

Usually, reflex smiles come and go sporadically, sometimes even while the baby is napping or feeling tired. But a genuine smile, you will see in their eyes— the emotion will shine through when they respond to your appearance or a sibling's voice. These smiles are more consistent and come as a reply or response to positive interaction, yet another reaction to visual and vocal stimuli.

Although we take this as a cheerful sign, smiling means a lot more than you think. When your baby gives you one of those cute toothless grins, it is a good sign that their vision has developed well enough for them to recognize you on sight. That little brain has improved enough to discard reflex smiles and shows that the nervous system has also appropriately developed through this new sign of control.

Following up on smiling, let me also include one of the most adorable happenings you will encounter for the first time at this stage—cooing. You may realize that baby's facial expressions directly correlate to the mood of the moment as you chat or sing, adapting to the tone of your voice and reacting accordingly. This is where your baby will start returning the favor with a sound effect that is meant to tell you that they approve. Cooing is undoubtedly associated with conversation and contentment, quickly escalating to a humorous collaboration.

Most of all, cooing and smiling displays a baby's emotional growth and their ability to articulate demeanor and happiness. The sweetest part is how they revel in the reaction their smiles get from you and those around them who respond to their expressions. This is, without a doubt, a wonderful way for your baby to start having an emotional exchange with others.

SKIN-TO-SKIN

Skin-to-skin contact refers to placing the undressed baby directly on the parent's chest so that their skin is touching. This is a crucial part of developing a bond with your child. We usually direct advice toward the mothers, but the baby needs to have some skin time with the other parent as well!

In fact, skin contact with the father is equally vital for a baby's brain to mature and promote better sleep through cuddles. After all, there can never be too much cuddling, right? Cuddling with dad adds to baby's growth on a scientific level. This multi-sensory experience accelerates essential neurological pathways to encourage brain development, and research shows that babies who are carried like tiny kangaroos sleep better and exhibit less stress response. Immune function and digestion improve because of an exchange between dad and baby's anti-bodies and elevate the release of efficient hormones to help with good metabolism. Therefore, your baby's body finds it more comfortable to absorb essential nutrients when their chemical levels are ideal.

Before I end this chapter, let's look at some issues you may feel concerned about but are usually nothing to worry about.

CROOKED FEET

If you are worried about your baby's oddly bent legs and feet, relax. Think about it—your baby was scrunched up in your womb for nine straight months and had very little wiggle room! Like a little wrapped package, their legs and feet have had to fold inward to accommodate them, so it is natural for a baby's legs and feet to seem crooked at first. Crooked feet will correct themselves in the next months as they kick about in the air, but you are welcome to help them along with some easy massaging techniques.

Hold your baby's feet in the palm of your hands. You will see how they are slightly curved to the inside. Gently hold the heel and use your fingers to stretch your baby's foot out until it looks straight. If this happens effortlessly with a few gentle stretches, you can rest assured that it is only temporary, and their feet will correct themselves in the following months. Keep doing these stretches to help the correction if you wish.

Now, if you are still not sure if this is normal in your baby, check for symptoms that might display a possible problem, such as a deep crease in baby's soles or a bigger curve in the front part of their feet.

Also, note the flexibility of your baby's feet after you do the stretches mentioned above, and if the foot does not respond as it should, speak to your doctor.

PENILE ADHESION

You might hear about penile adhesion from other parents of boys.

It is normal for the skin of the penile shaft to be stuck to the head of a boy's penis (also known as the 'glans') in the first years of life. This is known as penile adhesion, which can occur regardless of circumcision. Usually, such adhesions are not painful or uncomfortable and vary in position and severity. In babies and young boys, such adhesions usually resolve themselves and do not need medical treatment.

This usually happens when there is excess foreskin after a circumcision, or it might occur if the foreskin is unable to retract in uncircumcised boys. As infants, some baby boys might develop adhesions if the child develops higher amounts of fat in the lower abdominal area or pubic region. Above the head of the penis, the fat pad grows prominently in infant years, which appears to swallow up the penis. This causes the skin to rub against the glans and might also cause irritation to the skin, so look out for mild rashes to the adhesion area.

INGUINAL HERNIA

Before I tell you how to spot it, let me tell you what to look for because an inguinal hernia does not show clearly in the first few weeks of a baby's life but is common in newborns.

Inguinal hernias can be seen as swelling in the scrotum or groin. The bulge normally comes and goes and can be particularly prominent after a baby has been crying. But what exactly is it?

While your baby is developing in your womb, his testicles form in his belly and descend via a tunnel to deliver them into the scrotum; baby girls also have this tunnel, known as the "processus vaginalis." Sometimes, this tunnel does not close and leaves an opening from the tummy into the inguinal canal, causing an ovary or section of bowel to get trapped in there. Basically, anything that should remain behind the abdomen can slip through and end up in the groin, from intestine to fluids. This condition can only be rectified with an operation to make sure there are no future complications that arise.

After knowing all this, I am sure you feel sated with knowledge and proud of yourself for making it this far already! Well done, you! As we both know, good sleep is still some weeks away, so just take it one step at a time. Remember to have your baby's vaccines up to date and get the doc to do a check-up for good measure and peace of mind! You will grow into this routine as much as your little one does, so be good to yourself and have fun with this new member of your family.

6

MONTH THREE

*S*till standing? Good for you, mommy; I knew you could do it.

Now, your baby has reached the extraordinary three-month mark, and you are in for some lovely changes in their physical and mental capabilities. Three months is a significant milestone in your baby's development. You will start noticing how they have shed the newborn rag doll essence, having matured considerably and probably expressing more than just the usual hunger pangs or wet diaper wails. It is good to explore what is coming next, not only to prepare but also to measure your progress so far. Comparisons help us to gauge performance and pat ourselves on the back for what we have already conquered, right? Without further ado, let us look at what is expected for the next month and how we can make the transition easy and productive.

MOTOR SKILLS, COMMUNICATION AND COGNITION, SENSES, SLEEP, AND GROWTH

What a mouthful! But hey, it is nothing we have not heard yet. In this next chapter, we will take these steps one by one to cover what is coming and what is expected during this time. Your bundle of joy will probably be able to arch that bobble-head right up to a 90-degree angle from all the tummy time exercises, and they should be laughing aloud and responding to your intentions, such as preparing to be picked up when you reach out to them. We will start with the basic senses and take it from there.

Vision

We know now that your baby's eyesight has locked on to primary recognition skills and perception of objects and movement, but their eyes are still adjusting. At month three, you can be sure that they can recognize you and others and distinguish between people more efficiently. You will now be able to level up to some more stimulating efforts during bath time or feedings and so on.

As their perception of colors improves, it would be a great idea to invest in a baby-safe mirror so that they can look at their expressions. You can also introduce a playing mat with lots of colorful items to promote focus and attention.

One of the things I loved most about month three is my babies' attempts to mimic my movements and expressions. It was extremely amusing.

Until now, your baby has not developed depth perception and tends to look at objects a bit cross-eyed. At three months, you should start to see some improvement in how they look at objects, judging distance without crossing their eyes.

Hearing

In the last chapter, we did not spend too much time specifically on hearing, but as the three-month mark is a milestone, you should know that your baby should actively respond to sounds at this stage. How do you test this? Just see if they react to a sound by turning their head toward the direction of the sound. They should also show signs of their ears measuring loudness by recoiling or startling at sudden, loud sounds or responding to softer sounds by looking toward the origin.

Grasp

As I have mentioned before, your baby's depth perception should be improving in comparison to last month. One of the best ways to ascertain this is to watch how they respond to grasping objects. As far as coordination, they should be grasping at objects with both hands and distinguishing between near and far a little better.

Sucking

If your baby is sucking their thumbs, don't worry. At this stage, it is perfectly normal to suck on their fingers as they become aware of their hands and fingers.

Scent

At three months, babies will start showing distinct preferences for smells and react to something they do not enjoy smelling by turning away. Even pleasant aromas will now draw their attention, just as their sense of taste improves. Remember that your baby is beginning to show personality by their reaction to sensory stimulation, making sure you do not have to keep guessing.

Standing Position

This is an inspiring time where your baby will not only show strength in their upper body and lifting their head better, but they will be developing overall muscle strength as well. At the three-month mark, your baby's knees, hip joints, and ankles will have considerably improved in power as well as flexibility. The range of motion in the body's joints will show by how your baby rotates onto and from their tummy or grasps their toes while on their back.

Hold your baby upright and see how firmly they plant those legs. You will be able to feel the support in your hands as your baby attempts to stand upright. Eventually, your little one will start doing that bounce to test the equipment, and the more you practice this with your baby, the sooner they will start getting in gear to try the walking thing!

Just like us, they need constant exercise to create stronger muscles and coordination.

FEEDING YOUR THREE-MONTH-OLD BABY

Correct adjustment of amount and frequency is instrumental in physical growth and immune function, so make sure to adapt your baby's feeding habits according to their needs. Timing changes according to how hungry your baby gets in relation to the frequency and contents of their nutrition. Of course, diet is as versatile as personality, and some babies will not need as much as others, or they might last longer before getting hungry. There are several aspects to cover in making minor changes, so let's explore them.

Nursing and Working

Most experts suggest that babies be fed whenever they are hungry. This is called feeding on demand, but at three months, the ideal timing sits at about every three to four hours to make sure a baby does not go too long without feeding. This is very important when it comes to putting on weight correctly.

If you are not sure how much your baby should be fed at every feeding, it is generally around 4-6 ounces. Of course, if you are returning to work, routines are sure to change, so adapt the feedings according to your combined schedule and find a reasonable middle ground where you can introduce gradual change. Whether you are using breast milk or are trying to wean baby onto formula, see what is best for both of you in terms of frequency.

Take note that sometimes babies cry for other reasons than hunger. Sometimes they just need a cuddle or a diaper change, but should they cry for a feeding, it is usually already late. Crying is their last resort when they have not been fed in time, so try to keep track of specific feeding times to make sure your baby does not have to cry to let you know they're hungry.

One critical point you should also note is that your baby will need larger amounts as they start gaining weight, so do not be alarmed if your baby seems hungrier than usual. It is just the metabolism catering to those growing bones and muscles.

Checkups are pivotal to keep track of your baby's nutritional adapting, so make sure you have them weighed and checked by the doctor on a regular schedule. This way, you can adjust feedings according to your baby's unique pace of growth because all babies are different in their speed of development.

Another overlooked point I would like to reiterate is hydration. Sometimes, we forget that babies need water as much as they need milk! Remember to keep your baby correctly hydrated and check their stool and urine to make sure that they get the right amount of nutrients and water. Clear or very light-colored urine is a good rule of thumb to measure your baby's water intake. As for poop, usually, it becomes lighter as they get older. Instead of the dark stool of newborns, their stool starts being more of a yellow or green.

Babies who breastfeed have a different consistency in their stool than babies on formula, so it is best to consider this before you stress about it.

Nighttime Feeding

At three months, most babies begin to sleep for longer stretches during the night, primarily if you feed them frequently enough during the day, and their tummies are satisfied by the time they go to sleep at nighttime. Now, don't panic if your baby is not sleeping as well as the norm suggests, which is usually about 10 hours. Your baby has their own needs and system of development. Be patient.

Do not forget that breastfed babies and formula-fed babies will differ in their feeding needs at night. Breastfed babies require approximately two to three night feedings, whereas formula-fed babies require one or two. Again, this is an estimation for optimal feeding, so adjust yours according to your baby.

As we pass the three-month milestone and we almost return to our regular schedules, most parents will feel that nighttime feeding should be gradually reduced as their baby starts sleeping for longer stretches at a time. Take note of your baby's night patterns and make sure that each feeding has the proper caloric substance. A true feed is estimated at two or more ounces per meal when the baby nurses for about four to five minutes. Anything less than this is considered not to be a true feed and might cause your baby to wake sooner than you want. Only with a proper intake of calories per meal will your baby have a comfortable sleep (and so will you). This will also prevent 'snacking' feeds—too many feeds with too little substance, adding up to way too many calories in total.

Where and how do you reduce baby's night feedings? Babies usually take their deepest naps during the first few hours of their night sleep, so you can start by initially reducing the earliest feed for the sole reason that your baby is more likely to fall asleep quicker after.

Using this rule of thumb, you should be able to adapt and choose which feeding to reduce since, in the morning hours, your baby is less likely to fall back to sleep easily. Choose whatever you're more comfortable with. If you are a night owl, you might prefer to reduce the 2 am feeding instead of the 11 pm feeding.

Something we don't always pay attention to is what our babies are wearing when they're ready for their nighttime sleep. Make sure that the temperature is even and comfortable to avoid your baby getting fussy and waking up for other reasons than feeding. Also, create a special space for nighttime sleep where your baby is surrounded by silence and darkness; the less distraction they have, the better they will sleep. The room should be cool, allowing your baby to regulate their body temperature to make their sleep more comfortable. This will promote sound sleep that might just lengthen the number of hours baby packs in for napping. Always great news.

Since we are on the subject of nighttime adjustments, please do make sure that baby is not swaddled anymore at this stage. It poses a great danger now that they are active enough to turn over on their bellies. We don't want a potential smothering situation, so keep your baby's arms free.

Sometimes your baby falls asleep while feeding. This happens for several reasons. Perhaps they are not getting enough milk and choose to fall asleep out of frustration. Often, they stop feeding and fall asleep because they get tired quickly. This might cause your baby not to get enough nutrition per feed and lead to more erratic sleep patterns. If your little one appears to struggle to get enough milk, consider changing breasts, or use breast compression to help.

It is not too worrisome, though, as babies' hormones are designed to make them sleepy after feeding. So, some of them tend to fall asleep already while still feeding, and this is entirely normal.

SLEEP SCHEDULE

By now, your baby is more settled into a schedule than those newborn weeks and should begin to adapt to their program of sleep based on feeding frequency, amount of wake time during the day, and quality of naps. Introducing a pacifier or safety toy or blanket should be in order at this stage to help your baby sleep without full attention from mom. As they all differ, babies should be urged to fall asleep more independently at this age, but a good schedule should ease the transition to longer sleep.

If you wish to keep track of the ideal sleep and wake times, feel free to use this example to gauge how close your baby keeps to what is ideal at three months old. Typically, at this age, they sleep between 14 and 17 hours a day, and this includes about four naps that add up to six hours, give or take.

For example, a typical daily sleep schedule could look like this:

- 7:00 am: Awake
- 8:30 am: Nap
- 9:30 am: Awake
- 11:00 am: Nap
- 12:00 pm: Awake
- 1:30 pm: Nap
- 3:00 pm: Awake
- 4:30 pm: Nap
- 5:30 pm: Awake
- 6:30 pm: Bedtime routine
- 7:00 pm: Bed

Nice and concise, right? See how close your baby keeps to this example to help you adjust where necessary. This sample is designed according to wake times of about 90 minutes and naps of one hour during the day, but of course, this does vary.

Bassinet to Crib

Another transition in the three-month milestone is when to move the baby from the bassinet to the crib. Obviously, if your baby has outgrown the bassinet, you should transition to the crib as the restrictive space could cause restless sleep. Most babies make the move at this age, but some might take longer (up to 6 months old). Younger babies are easier to transition from the bassinet to a crib because they are not as familiar with the bassinet yet. Therefore, it is better to move your baby sooner rather than later.

Then again, if your baby is comfortable still sleeping in their bassinet, maybe give it some time before moving them over to the crib.

ATTACHMENT

As you may have guessed, attachment is the bond that forms between a baby and their primary caregiver, usually the mother. This emotional bond is every bit as important as physical and mental development, and it runs both ways. Just as you and your partner feel a strong bond with your baby from the moment they are born, babies also get attached to you! (Remember that sweet smile you get when you enter the room?)

How this emotional attachment develops depends entirely on the attention your baby receives during their growth. Babies notice when and how you respond to them and are very sensitive to emotional reactions, so be aware of your tone and body language. We all have bad days, but it is vital to keep an even mood around developing babies in order to establish a loving and safe bond with consistency. Ever heard the term "quality time"? This is the secret to creating a sturdy attachment between you and your baby on a more casual level. Everyday play and attention do wonders not only for stimulation but also for learning to trust you.

Naturally, your baby cries when needing to be changed, fed, or cuddled, but they are keen observers of how quickly you respond. Have you noticed? Sometimes they appear downright impatient with your response time! How you respond to that crying spell forms a notion where they learn to trust you and depend on you for security. Safety is a strong bonding element that develops a powerful attachment between parent and child.

Having said that, make sure that your immediate attention does not spill over in 'spoiling' in later stages because overly attentive parents tend to teach a child that they are entitled to unnecessary attention, and this could develop into problematic behavior.

Make sure your baby knows that you are there for them when they need you to create an attachment of love and attention (attachment is nurtured by interaction and connecting). Once this attachment is established, you will notice that they are easier to console or soothe. You will realize that they want to be near you and close to you as much as possible, and this is an integral part of every aspect of caring for a baby.

Do you recall when we covered the chatting, playing, and singing to your baby? This is it! Holding them and talking to them is a sure way to form a powerful bond.

As discussed before, your baby needs as much dad time as they do with mom, so make sure that they get equal amounts of bonding time with both parents. Parental bonds are more important than any other bond baby might form with family members or caregivers.

BREATHING: LAPSES AND EMERGENCIES

We do not like to think of possible problems arising, but we have to be prepared for them. To make sure that you react quickly enough, it is best to learn the signs of potential threats to your baby. Make sure you understand how baby's breathing usually sounds and recognize the patterns. This way, you will quickly be able to identify any inconsistencies. Familiarize yourself with your baby's breathing so that you will be able to explain any oddities to the pediatrician. Up to 29% of all neonatal intensive care admittance is due to respiratory distress, and there are symptoms to listen for in order to make sure the proper treatment is employed should such a problem arise (Sexton & Natale, 2009).

Whistling noise could be a blockage of the nostrils, but your pediatrician will be able to advise you on how to suction mucus gently.

Another sound you might find could be a barking cough or a hoarse cry. This is usually due to some form of windpipe blockage from mucus or perhaps inflammation in the voice, like croup, which is exacerbated at night.

If your baby presents a deep cough, it could be a sign of blockage of the large bronchi. Your baby's doctor will be able to get a better listen with a stethoscope to confirm.

Most babies who wheeze might exhibit a more severe condition. Wheezing is a sign of the narrowing or blocked lower airways caused by several possible conditions, such as asthma, pneumonia, or a respiratory syncytial virus.

Although babies breathe faster than older children, rapid breathing could mean fluid in the airways. Pneumonia is one such infection that results in fluid in a baby's airways. If a baby breathes unusually fast, it could also be because of fever or infection and should be assessed immediately.

If your baby is snoring, it could result from something less problematic, such as a stuffy nose, but in worse cases, snoring could be a sign of enlarged tonsils or sleep apnea. A constant and high-pitched sound could indicate an obstruction in the airways, such as laryngomalacia, but make sure by asking for your doctor's opinion, just to be safe.

If your baby grunts while breathing, emitting a low noise when breathing out, it could signal a lung issue or some severe infection, so it would be best to get to the doctor immediately.

Ultimately, it is best to remain calm if you suspect that your baby could be in trouble. Look at your precious angel to see if they are in distress if they are breathing irregularly. This could be alarming for any parent, but you can never be too careful. Always feel free to contact your physician if you suspect something might be wrong.

Preventative measures are always a good rule. Make sure your baby always sleeps on their back to decrease the risk of sudden infant death syndrome (SIDS), and do not prop them up in their crib. Instead, obtain some medical advice on how to effectively clear congestion. You might want to invest in some saline drops that you can buy over the counter at pharmacies. These are very efficient in loosening thick mucus.

As mentioned before, make sure your baby is dressed comfortably in breathable fabric to keep them from overheating. This, too, can cause rapid breathing, so ensure that your baby's body temperature stays constant.

If your baby exhibits blue-colored nails or lips, it could be a sign of oxygen deprivation. Check if your baby doesn't breathe for 20 seconds or longer and call the emergency response immediately. Instant response is also required if your baby is grunting at the end of every breath, breathes with flaring nostrils (struggling to get enough oxygen), or becomes lethargic in addition to having trouble breathing.

WORKING PARENTS

When deciding when to work while taking care of a baby, balance is the key. Like so many other working moms, you might feel some intense detaching anxieties when faced with your new routine of returning to work, but you should not feel stressed about it. After all, it is all part of the next exciting step in juggling work and motherhood! Take it easy on yourself.

It might be great to know you are returning to an adult environment at the office, but you will be just as excited to get home after work to see your baby again. It's all good. Most moms struggle with a feeling of guilt when they go back to work, but this is not warranted, especially if you spend quality time with your bouncing bundle of joy when you are home. You might even feel spread thin between being needed at both work and home, but give yourself a break—it only means that you are important. It is not easy for anyone to give a hundred percent in both worlds, but it will get better as you get used to the routines together.

What makes it even better on your emotions is to have a caregiver you trust, someone you know is giving your baby all the attention and thorough care they need. If you have a partner, even better! After all, if you do not have to worry about the baby, it is easier to concentrate on your job. Dividing responsibilities alleviates a great deal of stress and helps both mom and dad cope with their other jobs. Routines are essential to ease back into the work environment. Make sure your mornings are more leisurely by implementing a routine to make things as fluid as possible. Doing the same chores every day should create more harmony.

As you start your new routine between work and home, the obvious question is always what kind of daycare would be best for the baby. You have plenty of options, so do your homework and choose what is best for you and your baby. Here are some possibilities.

In-Home Care

You could opt for in-home care, which is best when you prefer to have your baby at home all day while you are out to work. A lot of grandmothers love to offer this specific opportunity. Still, you can always hire a caregiver to take care of your baby at home if you do not want to uproot their surroundings and shove them into an unfamiliar environment.

Babysitter

A wise rule of thumb when hiring a babysitter is to make sure that they have basic CPR and medical knowledge. No, you don't have to employ Dr. Quinn, but it helps to hire someone responsible who could minimize possible problems.

Hiring a Nanny

First, determine what you want from your nanny and take note to put this in your requests. Needless to say, the most important part of hiring a nanny is to get solid references and a background check to make sure that your choice of nanny comes with peace of mind.

It is imperative that you employ a babysitter or nanny who is reliable and does not have any habits detrimental to your baby. Nanny cams are extremely popular for this very reason and help you keep an eye on your babysitter while you are out. This might sound insidious, but your baby's welfare is more important than anything. Apart from nanny cams, you can look out for habits that might harm your baby, such as smoking, having friends come over while babysitting, or alcohol or drug use.

Even something as small as ignoring your orders or requests should give you second thoughts because essentially, this person is in charge while you are absent.

Group Daycare

Most babies and younger children under three do better with home-based childcare than group daycare because it includes more personal attention. Understandably, if group daycare is the only option, it is not the end of the world. Just consider the size of the group to ensure that the attention is divided between not too many children.

Corporate Daycare

Once again, I do not recommend external daycare for a three-month-old, but if this is what you have to use, there are some outstanding incentives for using corporate daycare. Having your baby inside your work environment might make you feel less apprehensive since you are in close vicinity, so if your company offers daycare, you might like this option sheerly for the convenience of it.

As always, let's end this chapter with some health issues that may arise.

DIAPER RASHES

The first time you encounter your baby's sore, reddish bum, you are bound to be concerned, but diaper rash is quite typical and is caused by several factors. Obviously, if the rash continues or develops into something more substantial, you should speak to your doctor.

Usually, rashes are triggered by enzymes in poop, and this can irritate their skin. Typically, wet skin and friction from the diaper cause reddish irritation, but sometimes yeast can cause a rash too. As you know, yeast develops best in warm, wet environments, and what better place than that warm, moist diaper, right?

On top of this, there are other irritants like bath products, urine, or laundry detergents, so it is almost par for the course to see that bottom with the occasional rash.

PENIS SORES

When you have a baby boy, there are always concerns when the penis is sore or inflamed. There are several causes of various conditions, such as foreskin infections or balanitis. Balanitis has symptoms such as tenderness, itching, or pain on the glans or red sores on the penis or the skin around the head of the penis. There might also be a thick, smelly discharge on the head of the penis, or your baby could have trouble urinating. Make sure this gets treated as soon as possible; otherwise, the penis could swell or the (uncircumcised) baby's foreskin could stick to the glans and form scars.

SHAKEN BABY SYNDROME

Yes, that's a thing, so be very wary of your mood when you handle your baby. Most of the time, this occurs when someone shakes a baby violently, usually in frustration, if a baby won't stop crying. This can cause substantial brain damage because babies have weak muscles in their necks that already impair the support of their head. Therefore, shaking a baby will cause their head to shudder uncontrollably and thrashes that little brain against the inside of the baby's skull. This could cause swelling and bleeding, which are deadly.

After covering all the new factors that come with your maturing baby at this three-month mark, you should be well equipped for the next few weeks! Now that baby is a bit more human you should find that routine turns to habit.

～

7

MONTH FOUR

Get ready for fun, games, and a lot of talking. In month four, your baby wants to be social with anyone and everyone. Your house will fill with laughter as your little one starts to get to know their personality and shares it with you in such delightful ways. Your baby will really begin to shine during this month as they begin to express their emotions more easily.

One of the most noticeable physical changes is that your baby will have doubled their birth weight by month four. In general, babies will weigh at least 13 pounds at this age. However, if your baby was a preemie, they may need some extra time to catch up.

Your little one should be able to raise up on their arms during tummy time and may even roll over and reach for an object. When propped into a sitting position, they should be able to keep their head level. You will also notice that your baby's legs are getting significantly stronger, and they will be able to bear weight on their legs when you hold them upright.

One of the things I found the most adorable was when my little girl would play with her toes. She even sucked on them at times. If this happens, don't worry, it's perfectly normal during this time. Babies tend to see toes as built-in toys!

Some of the babies who are more advanced in the milestone department may even be able to sit unassisted as well as stand up while holding on to someone.

One of the most important things for you to do during this month is to listen to your baby. Your little one will be babbling away, and you will hear more vowel and consonant combos. Their ga-ga-ga and ba-ba-ba will soon turn into mama and dada, and I know that is one thing you can't wait to hear.

Here's a quick list of all the developmental milestones you can expect at this age.

Your baby should be able to:

- Roll over onto their back when placed on their tummy
- Sit without support
- Bear weight on their legs
- Hold up their head
- Hold baby toys and rattles
- Push up when on the stomach
- Reach for objects
- Follow moving objects with their eyes

The development in your tiny one's brain is also worth noting:

- Learn cause and effect
- Understand object permanence—blanket, toys, and other objects don't disappear; they're just out of sight
- Improved eyesight and enhanced visual perception of patterns, shapes, and colors
- Express negative emotion
- Mimic facial expression
- Recognize people
- Cry in different ways to communicate

hunger, frustration, sleepiness, and
boredom

Since your baby will need a lot of stimulation and
entertainment from this month onward, you will
have to experiment with new activities and use new
equipment to keep them busy. Here are some of the
things I did to keep my babies' minds and bodies
occupied:

- Use hanging toys or mobiles for them to
  reach for
- Take them on walks in a stroller so that
  your baby can see what is going on
  around them
- Play peekaboo
- Read a book. I know you think your four-
  month-old baby won't understand, but your
  voice, as well as the bright colors in the
  books, will be stimulating to look at.
- Place your baby on their tummy with toys
  scattered out in front of them. This will
  keep them entertained as they try to reach
  their toys.

I also recommend you use mirrors. As mentioned, your little one is very sociable during this time, and they want to see faces—it doesn't matter if it is their own! I used to sit cross-legged on the floor with my baby in my lap and show them their reflection. When you point and touch specific areas of their face, they'll make the connection that it is their face they're seeing. If you have more than one child, this is an excellent way to get siblings to bond.

You can also fasten a mirror (unbreakable) to the side of your little one's crib to keep them entertained for hours on end.

Don't forget that you're going to have quite the conversationalist on your hands. If you see that your little one is not talking a lot, you can do a few things to get them talking:

1. Ask them questions...and then answer them. I know you're talking to yourself, but you're modeling the structure of a conversation.
2. When your baby starts talking, take the time to pay attention. Look at them as they tell you long and intricate stories you can't

understand. They will appreciate this attention. Furthermore, you'll notice how hard they're working at mastering their 'mmm' and 'ahhh' sounds.

3. If you don't have a topic to talk about, just repeat what you and your little one are doing. "I'm warming Allie's bottle to get her tum-tum nice and full."

4. When you hear a noise, point it out to your baby. You want your little one to have "listening ears" as they grow into toddlers—that is to say, ears that will hear and heed your rules! So, get them to notice various sounds and hone those listening skills.

5. Grab a book and read to your tiny tot. Books make great sources of new words and may even instill a future love of reading in your baby.

6. Mimic your baby's sounds as they make them, and you will soon find yourself discussing the secrets of the universe for hours (even though only your baby will understand them).

FEEDING YOUR FOUR-MONTH-OLD BABY

Your little one will be catching a lot more z's than you're used to, so you may not be feeding as much as the previous three months. A four-month-old baby will be eating six to seven ounces every four to five hours when formula-fed. If you're breastfeeding exclusively, you can expect your baby to nurse six to eight times in 24 hours. At times when your baby goes through a growth spurt or when they're sick, you can expect them to be hungry more often.

You may, at this time, be thinking about introducing solid food. Although doctors in the past believed that the four-month mark was a good time to add solids, experts now believe that this is not set in stone. Some babies may be ready to try solid food at this young age, while others will not be ready until they're seven months or older (Mayo Clinic, n.d.).

You will know your baby is ready for a change when they no longer use their tongue to push solid food out of their mouth. This will show that they have developed some coordination to move food from the front of the mouth to be swallowed.

According to The American Academy of Pediatrics (n.d.), you can look for the following signs that your baby is ready to try solids:

- Your little one can hold their head up when sitting in a feeding chair.
- Your baby opens their mouth like a baby bird when food comes their way.
- Your baby mimics you when you eat or reaches for your spoon when you're eating in front of them.
- Your little one makes an effort to move food from a spoon into their mouth.
- They have doubled their birth weight or weigh at least 13 pounds.

When you do decide to start your baby on solid food, bananas, avocados, sweet potatoes, and single-grain baby cereal should be on top of the list of choices. Just keep in mind to start slow—one or two ounces at a time is more than enough. Also, should your baby not want to finish the food, don't force it. You can introduce a new food every few days to give your baby's tummy a chance to get used to the solids, but keep an eye out for signs of a food allergy.

To recap, here is how much your little one should eat when they're four months old.

Formula: Four ounces, four to six times a day.

Breastfeeding: Your baby will typically want to nurse every three or four hours. When your baby seems content and your breasts feel soft and empty, then you'll know that your little one has had enough. Keep an eye on their weight; if they keep gaining weight healthily, you're breastfeeding an adequate amount. To give you an idea, women who pump breast milk will notice that their baby will drink about 25 ounces per day. This amount should then be divided between how many feedings your little one typically has during the day. You can also check how many diapers you use per day—a healthy baby who is getting enough milk will go through about four to five very wet diapers per day.

Breast Rejection

Your baby may go on a "nursing strike" unexpectedly. This can be caused by several reasons. It may be possible that your baby is teething, and this makes sucking painful, or they may be suffering from a cold, which makes it difficult to breathe through the nose.

Other reasons include:

- Earache
- The food you ate
- Stress and tension

Breast rejection may also happen for no apparent reason at all, but don't worry, it's often temporary.

One thing your baby's nursing strike won't be is self-weaning, so don't confuse the two. It is unlikely that a four-month-old baby will be ready to wean. This usually only happens close to your little one's first birthday. Your baby's breast strike won't be permanent.

BABY'S SLEEP

When it comes to your baby's sleep pattern, you may feel somewhat confused. Where your little one once slept soundly except for waking for feedings, your four-month-old may not be such a good sleeper anymore.

This is termed "sleep regression" and happens because your baby's brain is much more active than it used to be. This new alertness means they may wake up crying during the night, and you can expect to have your sleep disrupted two to three times a night. Four-month sleep regression luckily only lasts for two to six weeks, but one way to get your baby to sleep more deeply is to set up a routine. Also, I know you may not be too happy to read that getting your baby used to sleeping in their crib and not your arms is best. But it really is.

Most babies this age will sleep 15 hours a day—10 hours during the night and two or three daytime naps to cover the remaining five hours. My three babies all had a morning nap and a longer afternoon nap. During very busy days, they even had a quick evening nap.

Sleep Training

You can also start to sleep train your baby during this time. I can just imagine your face if you haven't heard about sleep training before, but don't worry, it doesn't include any leashes or treats. However, the process will help your little one learn how to fall asleep and sleep longer. If you dig a little deeper, you will see that sleep training is a controversial topic, but if you've learned anything in this book, there is no one right way when it comes to babies.

One thing is sure, the benefits of training your baby to sleep are significant—everyone in your home will be well-rested, and your baby will continue to grow nicely since sleep is essential to their development (Dahl, 2007).

You can take different approaches to train your baby to sleep, with these being divided into more 'gentle' sleep training or the 'extinction' label. As I said before, there is no right or wrong method—it all depends on your family and circumstances and what works for you. Sleep coaches can help you, but I will list the more common approaches to give you an idea of what to expect.

No tears: This is also known as the no-cry method. You will subtly work on your baby's sleep habits. For example, if your little one likes being rocked, you will reduce the time you rock until it is not necessary for any rocking. Substitution also falls under the "no tears" method, where you will switch out the routine. For instance, if your little one is used to getting fed before bedtime, read them a book instead.

Cry it out: I realize that this method is not for everyone. It can break your heart to hear your baby crying as they self-soothe trying to get to sleep. That being said, your baby can learn to calm themselves, stop crying, and sleep through the night.

Weissbluth method: If you like routines, then this may be the method for you. But be warned, it does have a self-soothing component. When it is sleep time, set up a routine—bed, reading, lullaby, sleep, as an example. Once the routine is completed, close your baby's room door and don't open it until the next morning. If you have a baby monitor, have a look at it, and you'll see that soon your baby will suckle their thumb and fall asleep. At first, it may take an hour, but it may be 20 minutes or less as the training progresses.

Ferber method: For some parents, this is a comfortable midway if they don't want to completely ignore their baby. It is a form of graduated extinction sleep training where you'll be able to check on your baby at various time intervals after putting them down for sleep. You're not allowed to pick your baby up, but nothing stops you from saying a calming word or giving them a soothing pat on the back. The intervals will get longer as you go until your baby is sleeping throughout the night soundly.

Chair method: You will start with a chair next to your baby's crib. Each night, move the chair farther away until you're no longer in the room. You're allowed to pick up your little one occasionally but try to avoid it as much as you can. This method is perfect for babies who suffer from separation anxiety. It will show them that mommy and daddy aren't gone, they're just on the other side of the door.

Pick up and put down: This is the most common sleep-training method. You will put your baby to bed while awake and check on them regularly and even pick them up when they're upset. Your little one will become drowsy throughout the process and fall asleep on their own.

SIT UP, LITTLE ONE

Your baby has been spending a lot of time on their tummy or relaxing in a reclining position. When they turn four months old, it is time for a change of scenery. Although some babies will be ready to sit propped up at three months already, it will take most a month longer. As soon as you see that your little one can hold their head up without any trouble, you can help them sit by propping them up with some pillows or other support.

I suggest that you put your little one on a soft blanket or close to you if they topple over. We don't want any injuries. If you find that your baby slumps over or falls to the side often, even with support, it may be a sign that they're not quite ready to reach this milestone yet. Simply try again later.

The more practice your baby gets holding themselves upright with some assistance, the sooner they'll sit independently. This will give them a better perspective of the world and, of course, their favorite people —mommy and daddy!

It is vital to give some form of support as most babies' heads will fall backward when seated upright. One way to strengthen your little one's neck and head is by playing a game of pulling them into a sitting position. So, when your little one is on their back, take hold of their hands and gently pull them up to sit. I know my little girl enjoyed this game tremendously. Another way to work those neck muscles is to take your baby for regular walks in a stroller through the neighborhood. Point out interesting things for them to look at to develop their interest in sitting.

The more you help your baby practice their sitting, the more likely they are to try sitting up on their own. Babies are inquisitive little things—the more they discover the world from their vantage point, the more they'll try to do it without mom or dad's support.

Even if your baby can't sit with support when five months old, don't worry! Your baby will do things at their pace. Relax about reaching specific milestones at specific times, just make sure to keep the encouragement going.

CAR SEAT TROUBLES

Your baby won't be happy about being strapped into a car seat, so it is vital that you get it right from the beginning. Still, some babies just can't help but become upset the minute you place them in a car seat—and they won't calm down quickly either. To start strong and get them used to riding in a car seat, there are a few things you should and shouldn't do. For one, when you lean your little one back into the seat, make sure the straps are pushed to the side. Feeling these straps push into their back is sure to cause discomfort, which will reinforce their hatred of this confining space. You will have to juggle your baby with one arm while you maneuver the car seat straps out of the way.

It is also worth trying to create a positive association with the car seat. You can sit in the back seat and play a game or two with your baby while they are strapped into the seat. Music or white noise also works wonders. Experiment with different sounds— avoid loud noises and opt for soothing music instead. Talking or singing will also let your little one know that you're still there, and there's no need for them to panic.

SUCKING AND TEETHING

Babies like sucking on things because it reminds them of the time they were all snug and safe in your womb. Five womb sensations can trigger your baby's internal calming reflex, and sucking is one of them (Karp, n.d.).

You won't believe the relaxing effect sucking has on babies. It lowers their heart rate, blood pressure, and even reduces crying after those dreaded vaccinations and any blood tests.

Newborns may not suck their fingers as often as they'd like because their muscle coordination is still poor. This is why they're so relieved when given a pacifier, breast, or bottle.

When your little one sucks on a toy or their thumb, we call it non-nutritive sucking—it adds no nutritional value. This type of sucking, however, has a relaxing effect on your baby. Think of it as baby meditation. It helps your little one keep calm while they're getting used to the chaos in the world around them.

Benefits of Pacifiers

I know you may be worried about giving your baby a pacifier because you feel it's habit-forming. The good news is sucking for babies isn't like candy or an addiction; it is a fundamental part of the fourth trimester and a step closer to your baby's self-reliance.

According to pediatricians Sexton and Natale (2009), parents should give their newborn a pacifier from one month old and up. If you're bottle-feeding your baby, they can sleep with a pacifier right after birth. On the other hand, breastfed babies should only be given a paci once nursing is going well.

It's okay if the binky turns out to be your baby's best friend; there are many benefits to sucking on a pacifier. For one, it is very calming to them, but even more extraordinary is that sucking a pacifier when taking a nap can lower the risk of sudden infant death syndrome (SIDS) (Karp, n.d.).

When it comes to teething, you can rule it out for the first three months of your newborn's life. However, if your older baby is a little more irritable than usual, drooling buckets, and not sleeping as soundly as usual, you can probably assume they're teething. You may also notice that they're sucking on anything they can find. This is because their gums are sore, and rubbing something against them makes it feel somewhat better. This is not a fun phase of your baby's growth, and you can expect a lot of tears—even runny stools. The whole family will get through it!

BABY WEIGHT

For doctors to determine if babies are reaching their physical developmental milestones, they use weight as a measure. When your little one doesn't gain weight at a normal rate, it may indicate that there are underlying health issues, and not picking up weight is concerning because it may stunt your baby's growth. Furthermore, it may negatively impact their immune system.

But what exactly affects your baby's weight? Well, it is determined by many factors, including:

Genetics: Size of each of the birth parents.

How long you were pregnant for: If your baby was born before the due date, they most likely would be smaller than average. Conversely, if they were born past their due date, they may be larger.

What you ate during pregnancy: A healthy diet plays a vital role in your baby's development inside your womb and beyond.

Lifestyle habits: Smoking, drinking alcohol, or taking drugs while pregnant can drastically affect your baby's birth weight and development.

Your baby's gender: Boys are usually larger than girls.

Mother's health: If mommy has diabetes, high blood pressure, heart disease, or obesity, it may affect her baby's weight.

Number of babies: The more babies in the womb, the more their weight will be affected. It's all about how much space they have to share.

Birth order: Your firstborn will be smaller than their brothers and sisters.

Baby's health: When your baby has any congenital disabilities or other medical issues, it may impact their weight.

Babies may have a hard time gaining weight for the following reasons:

- They struggle to suckle.
- They're not getting fed enough times during the day, or their calorie intake is too low.
- They can't stomach milk.
- They were exposed to a prenatal infection.
- They suffer from cystic fibrosis or other birth defects.

Similarly to underweight babies, little ones who carry extra weight require close medical attention. Doctors need to keep an eye on these babies' sugar levels. Should your baby gain weight rapidly in the first six to 12 months, don't be alarmed. This is especially common in breastfed babies, and the weight gain will slow down after a while.

One thing to keep in mind is that overweight babies may start to crawl and walk later than other babies. Overall, it is best to keep your baby at a healthy weight as it will also eliminate weight issues later on in their life.

POSSIBLE HEALTH ISSUES

Here are some health issues you need to keep an eye out for in month four of your little one's life.

Heart Murmurs

If you listen to your heartbeat, you'll hear a lub-dub, lub-dub sound. However, the blood in some people's veins is extra noisy as it courses through the heart. This is what is called a murmur. It is essentially a whooshing sound that doctors pick up between heartbeats. Heart murmurs are common, and most kids have them at some point. Should your baby's doctor feel that the murmur points to possible problems with the heart, they will refer your child to a pediatric cardiologist who will conduct various tests, including:

- Chest X-ray
- EKG
- Echocardiogram

Those babies born with a structural heart problem or some heart defect will show signs a few days after birth or later on in life. Furthermore, some will only have a heart murmur, while others will show symptoms, including rapid breathing, difficulty feeding, blue lips, and overall failure to thrive.

Common heart defects include septal defects, valve abnormalities, outflow tract obstruction, and heart muscle disorders.

Black Stool

If your baby's diaper is filled with thick, black stool, it often indicates bleeding in the digestive tract. As you can imagine, this is dangerous for your little one. Before your baby turns three months old, they will have what are called meconium bowel movements, which will be black but not dangerous. Also, before you get worried, check if the formula you're feeding is iron-fortified or whether you're supplementing with iron. This will turn stool dark brown or black.

8

MONTH FIVE

This month is a month of transition. Doctors usually don't measure developmental milestones during this month, but there are a wide range of highlights that you'll notice at this time.

You're one month away from celebrating your baby's first six months on the planet—that's half a year! I am sure by now you two have slipped into a routine, and you are more at ease when it comes to looking after another life.

If you and your little one's day don't start early in the morning, I recommend you adapt it a little. The best time to spend together is in the morning. Your baby is their most active and happy then, making it the perfect time to strengthen your bond further. Your baby is a sponge, and they will absorb everything that is going on around them. So, join them on their level. Plop down next to them on the floor and have fun!

This is also the time the groundwork for language begins, and you should try to make an effort to have as many conversations with them as possible, read to them, and even play some music—grownup music.

MILESTONES

Let's have a closer look at the developmental milestones you can expect at month five.

Body

- Rolls onto stomach or back.
- Can sit with support. May push into a sitting position all on their own.
- Bears weight on legs.
- Reaches for toys and holds rattles comfortably.
- Can hold up their head and chest on their own.
- Can do tiny baby pushups by pushing to elbows from their stomach.
- Eyes are capable of following moving objects.

Brain

- Your baby is learning about cause and effect. For example, if they enjoy your reaction too much when they drop food off of the high chair, they might just do it again in the future.
- Your baby now knows that objects don't vanish forever when they are out of eyesight.
- Although your baby's eyes will only be

20/20 at six months, they have better eyesight than the previous months. They will also enjoy looking at shapes, patterns, and colors from this month on.

- They will smile at people and recognize familiar faces.
- Your baby will mimic facial expressions and language.
- There will be a distinct difference in your baby's cries from this month onward. You should be able to differentiate between a hunger cry, one of boredom or frustration, and a sleepy cry.
- Your baby will respond to your affection with a smile.

WHEN TO WORRY

As you've read numerous times throughout this book, babies develop differently, so you shouldn't worry too much if your baby misses a specific milestone. However, if your baby is displaying one or more of the following, talk to your doctor.

- Is cross-eyed.
- Hasn't gained 50% of their birth weight.

- Can't hold their head up.
- Can't sit up at all with support.
- Doesn't bring hands or other items to their mouth.
- Doesn't show interest in your face.
- Can't follow items that move with their eyes.
- Isn't smiling.

FEEDING YOUR FIVE-MONTH-OLD BABY

It is time for you to consider switching your little one over to solid baby food. Alternatively, you may decide to wait a while longer until your baby shows signs that they're ready (see the previous chapter for a refresher on the signs).

It isn't necessary for you to introduce solid foods in month six or even seven of your baby's life. Breast milk or formula contains all the nutrition your baby needs for the first half-year. What I enjoyed most about moving my babies over to solid food was the opportunity to make my own baby food. It saved me a lot of money, but even more importantly, I could offer my angels fresh and nutritious food without any preservatives.

As a side note, when you start feeding your baby solid foods, you have to adjust how much milk or formula you give. For example, when your baby first starts eating solid foods, they most likely won't eat a lot and will still rely primarily on milk.

How to Introduce Solid Foods

Introducing solid food is all about getting your baby used to chewing and swallowing. For the first few days, it won't be about providing your little one with nutrition at all; instead, it will be about training them how to use their mouth in a different way. When you decide to add solid foods to their diet, continue to give your baby a breast or bottle in the morning and before bedtime. You can also add milk before or after meals that include solids. I recommend feeding your baby food first and then offering them milk.

When your baby is comfortable chewing and swallowing solid food, start them on a routine where you offer them breakfast, lunch, and dinner. They may not always be hungry, but it will get them used to the idea of eating at specific times. But if your baby shows no interest in eating, don't force them.

· · ·

Allergies

One of the critical things to keep in mind about introducing solid food is to do so gradually, one food at a time. This isn't only to eliminate any food allergies but also to protect your baby's stomach from painful cramps. It doesn't matter in what order you introduce food; the important point here is to wait three to five days before adding another type of food. Don't make any other changes to your baby's diet while you're waiting to see if something you fed them causes an issue.

YOUR BABY'S SNOOZE BUTTON

Your baby will spend 11.5 to 14 hours in dreamland per day, and this will include two or three naps that range from 30 minutes to two hours. Your baby will most likely sleep through the night from the five-month mark. This may raise some safety concerns, especially since your baby can now freely roll from their stomach onto their backs but may find it difficult to move onto their backs from their tummy.

If you put your baby to sleep, always lay them flat on their back.

YOUR LITTLE ONE'S HEALTH AND SAFETY

Your tiny tot would have had their last check-up last month. If you missed it, don't worry, you can still schedule a visit for this month. This doctor's visit is crucial because it is time for your baby to get their second round of immunizations.

But other than vaccinations, there are some other things you will need to keep an eye on when it comes to your baby's health.

TEETHING

I briefly touched on teething in a previous chapter, but since your little one will start to cut teeth any day now, I want to share with you six things you should know about the process.

1. Teeth start to develop between six and 12 months.

There are a lot of variabilities when it comes to cutting teeth, and some babies still won't have teeth on their first birthday!

. . .

2. Add fluoride to your child's diet.

You've probably seen this mineral in your toothpaste. It plays an essential role in hardening the enamel of teeth and prevents tooth decay. This is why it is a good idea to give your baby fluoride when teething approaches. The best of it all is you won't have to spend any money on a supplement—good old tap water contains enough fluoride. Just make sure not to give your tiny tot too much! It can be toxic in large quantities, so always use no more than the size of a grain of rice.

3. Massage sore gums.

While it may not cause discomfort in some children, cutting teeth can be a painful process. To help ease some of their distress, massage their gums, give them something cold to eat, or provide them with some acetaminophen.

4. Avoid tablets and gels.

I know it will be very tempting to offer some relief in the form of teething tablets, gels containing benzocaine, or even a teething necklace. All these pose a safety risk to your baby; the FDA has issued warnings against using benzocaine, and teething necklaces can cause strangulation and are a potential choking hazard.

5. Brush your baby's tooth/teeth.

Use fluoride toothpaste to strengthen your baby's teeth. Brush after the last drink or meal of the day.

6. Make a dental appointment.

As soon as you can see that little tooth poke through, phone to make an appointment with a pediatric dentist. He or she will make sure the teeth are developing as they should and that there aren't any dental issues. They'll also advise on proper hygiene. What I like most about making a dental appointment so early in your baby's life is the fact that they'll get used to visiting a dentist from a young age.

What Is a Teething Cough?

When your baby is teething, there will be an excessive amount of drool in their mouth as well as a constant drip down their throat. This oftentimes leads to what is known as a teething cough. To distinguish between a cough caused by teething, check for signs of nasal congestion. This extra symptom will point to the cough being a result of a cold, allergy, or something else.

Symptoms of a teething cough include drooling; fussiness; chewing; rubbing gums; loss of appetite; and swollen, red, and sore gums.

EAR PULLING

There are various reasons why your little one may be pulling on their ears. The main cause is usually because it became a habit as your baby touched and explored their face. Ear pulling as a habit usually happens between four and 12 months. When they're one year old, they'll have more interesting things to do.

Let's look at the other reasons why your baby may be tugging on their ear.

Earwax: Cotton swabs are too big for a baby's ears, and when used, they cause an earwax buildup in the ear canal. Your child should only use cotton swabs in their teen years—if at all—when the ear canal is wide enough for it. Until then, all you'll do when you use one on your baby is push the earwax back and cause further problems.

Soap: It's possible for soap, shampoo, or other irritants to get trapped in the ear canal.

Infection: If your baby is fussing, crying unexplainably, and acting sick, it may be an ear infection.

The bottom line is that simple ear pulling is perfectly harmless if no other symptoms like fever or crying are present. You should call your doctor when your baby keeps rubbing their ear for more than three days.

Eczema

Eczema is caused by an overreaction of your baby's immune system. Doctors have yet to pinpoint an exact cause, but they believe it is a mix of different things that lead to this condition. There are various allergens and bacteria that can trigger an eczema breakout.

But what is eczema, exactly? It's basically a genetic variation that affects the outermost layer of the skin and causes it to lose its ability to retain moisture and keep out foreign substances.

When it comes to treatment, there are various options, all consisting of four main goals:

- **Maintain a healthy skin barrier.**
  This is done by diligently sticking to a skin-care routine that helps repair the skin barrier.
- **Reduce inflammation.** Drink anti-inflammatory skin medication to reduce the inflammatory response during a flare-up. This step is not always appropriate for babies.
- **Control the itching.**
- **Manage triggers.**

There are also several ways to manage any flair-ups:

- **Give your baby a warm bath** for five to ten minutes. Apply moisturizer immediately after taking your baby out of the bath. Furthermore, avoid using any synthetic soaps or harsh and perfumed cleaning agents. Pay attention to how your little one's skin responds to frequent baths; some may do better with a good soak every other day. When you dry your baby after the bath, pat gently. This will leave some moisture on the skin over which you can then apply a moisturizer.

- **Use an ointment** if a lighter moisturizer is not doing the job. Look for something thick that will lock in the moisture and prevent your little one's skin from drying out. Always choose the most natural product—fragrances and preservatives can make eczema worse.

- **Identify your baby's triggers**, which is the most important aspect of managing your baby's eczema. You have to figure out what things in their environment trigger flare-ups or make them worse. It can be cleaning products you use in your home, non-breathable fabrics, sweat, pets, etc.

- **Apply a wet dressing** in the case of a severe flare-up to help skin stay moist. Your pediatrician will be able to explain how to do a wet dressing or use wet wrap therapy for eczema. At times, your doctor may prescribe a steroid cream to use with a wet dressing. You can apply a wet dressing for 24 to 72 hours until your little one's skin looks better.

- **Oral antihistamines** will help the itching that comes hand in hand with eczema. It is especially difficult to stop babies and children from scratching, so you will have to figure out a plan B. I suggest covering the skin with loose cotton clothing to keep them from scratching. Together with the clothing, give your baby an oral antihistamine to decrease the itchiness. Avoid applying an antihistamine cream as this will often worsen the flare-up.

The good news is that eczema usually gets much better as your baby grows up, and it may even go away entirely. Until then, talk to your pediatrician to develop a treatment plan to manage any flare-ups.

CHALLENGING BABIES

Is your baby difficult, or do you just feel that way because you find it challenging to be a mom at times? Don't worry, we've all been there—parenting is hard. The fact of the matter is one mommy's 'difficult' will be another's dream baby. You can imagine how this may make some women feel. They'll probably end up asking, what am I doing wrong?

This section is to put your mind at ease; you're not doing anything wrong. Sometimes you just have a high-need infant with a strong personality with different needs.

If you think about it, all babies are high-need babies in some or other areas in their life. But here are some characteristics of what some may call a 'challenging' baby.

They're intense: Some nurses will tell you in the hospital that your baby is going to be a handful. They can spot high-need babies in an instant. These little ones are usually the babies who protest when they're in the bassinet. They want to be one place only, and that is in their mother's arms. The cry of these babies are also easily distinguished from other babies— they're not making a request but an urgent demand! It's also possible to see a baby is intense by looking at their body language; clenched fists, tensed muscles, an arch backed, everything held in a "ready for action" way.

They're hyperactive: This characteristic is related to the intensity of a baby. For example, hyper-tonic babies are always in a tense state, as if they're ready to explode into action. Similarly, their minds are very seldomly in a relaxed state. One mother I talked to explained how she could tell her baby was 'hyperactive' from the moment she held her in the hospital. She didn't want to be swaddled and used to stiffen her limbs when faced with physical contact. These babies usually turn into gymnasts during breastfeeding as they arch their backs and do back-flips in your lap.

They're draining: High-need babies will tap the last bit of energy out of you and then ask for more. This is why many parents of such challenging babies use the term 'draining.' When you're an experienced mommy, you will operate in what many women call "the mother zone." This is where you're sleep-deprived, and everything feels a bit fuzzy, but you somehow get it right to function in low gear for a prolonged time.

They're demanding: As I mentioned above, high-need babies don't make requests; they demand feeding and holding, and they do it loudly. This often makes parents feel manipulated and controlled, and they may find it challenging to realize that it is just their baby's way of communicating.

Other words used to describe high-need babies include unsatisfied, unpredictable, and super sensitive. But whatever words are used to label these little ones, they remain special and deserve their space in this world. It may just require a bit more work and buckets full of patience from parents to meet their needs.

9

MONTH SIX

*O*kay, mommy, it is time to go bake a birthday cake and cut it in half for your now six-month-old baby. Can you believe you made it halfway through your little one's first year? And what a wonderful (and tiring) journey it has been so far. You'll be happy to know that this is the age where you will really start to enjoy your baby. Babies this age love to smile (and you can expect a toothy grin) and play and are just generally happy little beings.

Your baby will also start to recognize their name and may perk up and take note whenever you call them by their real name. Overall, your little one will be a real chatty Cathy, and you should make an effort to always respond to their very expressive conversation.

MAGIC MILESTONES

Things you can look forward to at this age include:

Body

- Can pass objects from one hand to another.
- Rolls from front to back and vice versa.
- Can sit without support.
- Bounces when standing (with support).
- Can put more weight on legs.
- Rocks on hands and knees.
- Can 'scoot' backward.
- Attempts to crawl.
- Starts using a raking grasp, which will progress to using their pointer finger and thumb (pincer grasp) over time.
- Can see across a room with ease.

Brain

- Sounds are tied to emotions.

- Will respond when talked to and will 'talk' back with sounds.
- Recognizes familiar faces.
- Recoils from strangers.
- Likes looking in a mirror.
- Can string together vowel sounds like 'eh,' 'oh,' and 'ah.'
- Will respond to emotions with sadness or happiness.
- Gets to know the world through taste and touch.

FEEDING YOUR SIX-MONTH-OLD BABY

If you haven't started introducing solid foods to your baby's diet yet, now may be the time. The important word to note is 'may' since some babies will only be ready in a month or two. I already covered the signs that your baby is ready for solid food, but let's quickly recap:

- Can hold head up.
- Mouth will open when food approaches.
- Food makes it into their mouth successfully and doesn't just land on their chin.

- Has doubled in birth weight or weighs at least 13 pounds.
- Shows an interest in food by reaching for a spoon or watching you eat.

You will find a bonus chapter at the end of this book containing some delicious homemade baby purees, which will work perfectly to introduce solid foods to your little one's diet.

If you plan on making your baby food, I feel it is important to share with you some foods you should not give your baby at this age.

Honey: Your baby must not be younger than 12 months before you give them honey. As you read earlier in this book, it may cause botulism in babies younger than a year.

Cow's milk: You can introduce cow's milk to your baby's diet when they have transitioned to solids successfully. Keep an eye on their tummy. They may still be too young to digest dairy at this stage, and it may cause microscopic bleeding.

Fish high in mercury: Although you can include fish in your baby's diet, you should not do so in excess. Whitefish, light tuna, and salmon are safe to give more often as they contain less mercury than other types of fish.

SLEEP

When it comes to your little one and their sleep, your baby should now be sleeping through the night as well as taking two to three naps during the day. That being said, it doesn't mean anything is 'wrong' when your baby isn't such a sound sleeper—they're probably just developing at a different timeline, or maybe they have different sleeping needs than other babies. Teething could also be the culprit stealing sweet z's from you and your little one.

The biggest change when it comes to sleep is that your baby will enjoy rolling from their back to their front. This is concerning to a lot of parents, but there is much less danger of SIDS at this age than there is in younger babies.

Although you should always put your baby in the cot on their back, it is not necessary to turn your baby back on their back should they roll over in their sleep. However, don't swaddle your baby from this point forward. As they get more active, swaddling poses a hazard. Similarly, don't leave any soft or loose bedding, blankets, or quilts in the bed. I suggest you use a sleep sack during winter to avoid heavy blankets your baby can become entangled in.

Early Risers

Even though your baby will be sleeping through most of the night, they may wake up bright-eyed and ready to play at 3 am when you'd prefer to stay in dreamland. This is not a biologically appropriate time for children to wake up so you have to resolve early rising issues.

There are four main reasons why your baby may be waking up too early:

- They're going to bed too late.
- They don't have enough naps during the day.
- They stay awake for too long between their afternoon nap and bedtime.
- They go to bed overtired.

To get your early riser to lie in a little longer, here are some tips.

1. Put them to bed earlier.

Keeping your child up late may actually cause early rising. Sounds counter-intuitive, I know, but when your baby is overtired, it will be difficult for their little body to relax enough to get to sleep. I suggest sticking to a bedtime between 7 and 8 pm.

2. Naps lead to better sleep.

I'm sure someone has told you that if you nap during the day, you're going to struggle to fall asleep at night. Well, the opposite is true for babies. The longer they're awake during the day, the more challenging it will be for them to get a good night's sleep, and they'll end up waking you up before the rooster.

3. Think about the wakefulness window.

This builds on the previous point. Your baby should not be awake for four hours at a time.

4. Rule out any medical conditions.

Your baby may suffer from sleep apnea, allergies, a cold, or GERD, which may all cause early rising. Any condition that restricts the nasal passageway will interrupt your little one's sleep. Babies, especially newborns, don't breathe through their mouths, so they won't sleep if something is blocking their airway.

Other than that, make sure they aren't hungry when you put them down. Most importantly, hang in there. Make a few small changes and see if they work. It takes time to change a sleeping habit.

10

BONUS: BABY FOOD RECIPES

*T*ime to put on your supermom apron so that you can serve your baby some culinary delights right from the start. Homemade baby food is all the rage at the moment, and I can understand why. You know exactly what your baby is eating. There are no hidden preservatives, additives, sugars, and other ingredients that aren't good for your little one.

Below are some tried-and-tested recipes made with wholesome products that will give your baby's tiny taste buds a spark of joy.

In fact, these purees are so delicious, I would be lying if I said I haven't eaten these purees alongside my babies! I shared these recipes with mommies who came to me for nutrition advice for them and their babies, and the reviews were nothing but positive.

Here are some reasons these mothers said they think homemade baby food is the way to go:

- It's freezer-friendly.
- You can make delicious purees using three ingredients or less.
- It's easy and quick to make.
- Purees are colorful and thus packed full of nutritional value.
- It's way cheaper than store-bought baby food.

Okay, let's get to the recipes. I want you to see, or better yet, taste why homemade baby food is superior.

Mango-Licious Puree

I don't know of a lot of people who don't like mango, and it is one of the world's healthiest fruits. This recipe is super quick, no-cook, 5-minute magic, and you'll only need one dish to make it.

Ingredients

- 2 cups mango
- 1 banana
- Pinch of nutmeg

Instructions

Mix it all up and give it a quick blitz to turn it into a puree.

Minty Asparagus Delight

This isn't a combination a lot of people will think of, but I promise you, your baby (and you) will enjoy it tremendously. It's ready in 20 minutes, and you can add it to your freezer stash for those grab-and-run moments.

Ingredients

- 12 oz asparagus
- 4 mint leaves

Instructions

Chop asparagus into rough chunks and steam. Once done, transfer to a blender and puree. Add the mint and give it another blitz. You can serve it to your baby immediately or spoon into freezer trays for later use.

Tip: Mix with chicken puree and cooked quinoa for a super nutritious baby dinner. Alternatively, serve with some ricotta or Greek yogurt.

Simple Chicken

This is a super basic baby food that you can add to any other purees for a protein and flavor boost.

Ingredients

- 1 8-oz chicken breast or thighs cubed (no bones or skin)
- 1 cup low-sodium chicken stock
- 1 tsp dried parsley

Instructions

Add the cubed chicken, broth, and parsley to a medium saucepan and bring to a boil. Turn the heat down and allow the chicken to simmer, covered, until cooked through. Let it cool slightly and use a hand-held blender to puree to your preferred consistency. You can add more stock if you feel it is necessary.

Creamy Sweet Butternut Squash and Cilantro

Your baby will love this one with its slightly sweet taste.

Ingredients

- 1 medium butternut squash
- ½ tablespoon cilantro (chopped)
- ½ cup water or broth (You can also use breast milk or formula.)

Instructions

Preheat the oven to 375 degrees Fahrenheit. Deseed the butternut and place on a baking sheet with the skin side down. Roast in the oven until tender when pricked with a fork. This can take anywhere from 35 to 45 minutes. Let the butternut cool slightly and proceed to scoop the flesh out to transfer to a blender. You can add the cilantro and puree until completely smooth. Add liquid until you reach a consistency you're happy with.

Apple and Cinnabon Puree

Your baby will go gaga over this one. It is delicious and nutrient-dense, which means your baby will get many vitamins and minerals while their taste buds do a little dance.

Ingredients

- 6 medium apples
- ¼ tsp cinnamon or to taste

Instructions

Peel and core the apples. Roughly chop the apples and place them with water and cinnamon in a saucepan. Turn the heat on medium-low and let it all simmer for 15 minutes. Transfer to a blender once cooked and puree until smooth.

You can serve or freeze it.

Thyme for Butternut Squash

This puree turns out creamy, smooth, and with a naturally sweet taste. The thyme adds a nice earthiness, which I'm sure your baby will enjoy.

Ingredients

- 1 butternut squash
- ¼ tsp chopped thyme

Instructions

Roast the butternut for 55 minutes, then give it a good blitz in a blender. Add the fresh thyme and continue to blend, adding liquid until smooth. You can serve it for your baby's next meal, or you can freeze it for later use.

Quinoa Baby Cereal

My middle boy loves the earthy taste of quinoa. Considering that it's loaded with protein, fiber, and magnesium, it is one of the ingredients I use often. You can serve it as a meal on its own or mix in a fruit or vegetable puree your baby also enjoys.

Ingredients

- 1 cup broth (You can use formula or breast milk if you want.)
- ½ cup quinoa

Instructions

Bring broth to a boil and add in the quinoa. Reduce the heat to a simmer, cover with a lid, and cook for 10 minutes. Once done, take it off the stove and let it stand for a further five minutes. You can then transfer everything to a blender and puree for two minutes. I like this puree to be completely smooth, so it will blend for a considerable amount of time. Remember, you're allowed to add extra liquid when things get a little chunky.

Green Bean and Basil Puree

Yummy! This is a great first to introduce your baby to. It's quick to make and has a deliciously mild taste to suit your baby's palate.

Ingredients

- 1 lb green beans fresh or frozen
- Fresh basil to taste (finely chopped)
- ½ cup reserved steamer water, formula, or breast milk

Instructions

Fill a medium saucepan with water and bring to boil. Trim the green beans and place into a steamer basket over boiling water. Cook until tender and let cool slightly. Keep the steamer water for later use. Add the green beans and basil to a blender and puree until smooth. Remember to add liquid if you're not happy with the consistency.

There you go; delicious recipes that are quick to make and jam-packed with all the nutrition your baby needs. I dare you to be adventurous. Think of combinations of ingredients you believe your little one will like, and give them a try!

LEAVE A 1-CLICK REVIEW!

I would be incredibly thankful if you could take just 60 seconds to write a brief review on Amazon, even if it's just a couple sentences!

SCAN QR CODE ABOVE OR VISIT LINK BELOW:
https://www.amazon.com/review/create-review/?&
asin=B08P9WY8FZ

CONCLUSION

Well, mommies and daddies, we've come to the end of *Our Plus One*. I hope you feel confident to bring your new bouncing baby home after reading this book. It truly is an amazing experience walking through your front door with an addition to the family. But it can also be a scary experience. As parents—especially new ones—we can't help but treat our newborn babies like fragile porcelain dolls who will break at the slightest touch. As you read in this book, that is far from the truth and can harm your little one. Some baby care basics even require you to work a little rougher to get the job done. Do you recall the nurse who gave a newborn a bath so rough one could easily mistake her for washing the dishes? She's a good example to follow.

Probably the most frustrating obstacle you'll face while raising your baby is not knowing what they want or need. But I can't end this book without telling you about how the deep bond you have with your baby will make communication more manageable—even without words. Yes, at first, you may not understand what your baby is 'saying,' but soon, you will develop your unique language. There's more to it than just crying. If you pay attention, you will notice that your baby uses various noises or cues to tell you what they need. Furthermore, knowing what to expect from birth to the six-month mark will make your life much more comfortable.

Of course, don't be so focused on the developmental milestones that you forget to pay attention to the smaller changes your little one will go through. In fact, I suggest you dust off that old video camera and start recording the remarkable changes your baby will go through. Parents are always quick to tell you that kids grow up so fast, and I don't want you to miss anything. You can start a baby journal, write your child letters to read when they're older, take weekly/monthly photos to document the physical changes, record them being their cute selves, or take up scrapbooking.

There's no doubt that this tiny human will change your life for the better, and you'll want to give them the best environment possible to grow into a happy and healthy toddler. But there's one point that I want to drive home as I end this book, and that is that you have to look after your health and happiness too. As mothers, we always put everyone else first, but that isn't good for anyone involved. It is time to realize that we can't share from our cup if there is nothing left in it. I know raising a kid doesn't leave much room for self-care, but I want you to make the time! Not just for you but for the rest of your family too.

My motto has always been that mothers are the glue of the family. That is why you need to look after yourself.

I hope this book did everything I wanted it to: leave you feeling calm and collected when you think about the day you bring your newborn home. You now have the knowledge needed to baby-proof your home, take care of your baby, and recognize the developmental milestones to look forward to as your baby grows.

If you enjoyed reading this book, please leave a review. I want to help mothers all around the world as they go through their pregnancy and afterward and have to learn to navigate the strange world of parenthood. Share with your friends and family members who are expecting. *Our Plus One* may just be the book they need to help them overcome any stress and worry about caring for their baby.

14 Baby Essentials Every Mom Must Have...

This checklist includes:

- 14 ESSENTIALS THAT YOU DIDN'T KNOW YOU NEEDED FOR YOUR LITTLE ONE AND YOURSELF
- ITEMS WHICH WILL MAKE BEING A MAMA BEAR EASIER
- WHERE YOU CAN PURCHASE THESE ITEMS AT THE LOWEST PRICE

The last thing you want to do is be unprepared and unequipped to give your little one an enjoyable and secure environment to grow up in. It is never too late to prepare for this!

To receive your free Mommy Checklist, visit the link or scan the QR code below:

https://purelypublishing.activehosted.com/f/1

ABOUT THE AUTHOR

Elizabeth Newbourne is an established nutritionist and loving mother of three. She has devoted her life to helping mothers understand how to take care of themselves and their little ones, both inside the womb during pregnancy and outside, as they guide their newborns through the developmental stages of life.

It is her passion to share with you everything she has learned from bringing into the world her two wonderful boys and her sweet little girl, as well as her two decades of knowledge in physical and psychological health and nutrition. She has coached and guided countless women through their pregnancies and helped mothers become the best version of themselves for their newborns and families, giving them access to the information she wishes she had when she was a new mother.

Her knowledge as a respected nutritionist, combined with her personal experience as a mother, makes her one of the leading experts on healthy and happy pregnancies and motherhood.

JOIN THE COMMUNITY:
www.facebook.com/groups/modernsupermom
www.instagram.com/elizabethnewbourne
elizabeth@newbornepublishing.com

REFERENCES

The American Academy of Pediatrics. (n.d.). Infant food and feeding. *AAP.org*. https://www.aap.org/en-us/advocacy-and-policy/aap-health-initiatives/HALF-Implementation-Guide/Age-Specific-Content/Pages/Infant-Food-and-Feeding.aspx

CDC. (2020). Recommended Child and Adolescent Immunization Schedule for ages 18 years or younger, United States, 2020. *CDC.gov*. https://www.cdc.gov/vaccines/schedules/hcp/imz/child-adolescent.html

CPSC. (2012). The tipping point: Highest number of TV and furniture tip-over deaths recorded by CPSC in 2011. *CPSC.gov*. https://www.cpsc.gov/Newsroom/News-Releases/2013/The-Tipping-

Point-Highest-Number-of-TV-and-Furniture-Tip-Over-Deaths-Recorded-By-CPSC-in-2011/

Dahl, E.R. (2007). Sleep and the developing brain. *Sleep.* https://www.ncbi.nlm.nih.gov/pmc/articles/PMC1978403/

Fletcher, J. (2019). Infant botulism: Symptoms, prevention, and recovery. *Medical News Today.* https://www.medicalnewstoday.com/articles/325626#:~:text=Infant%20botulism%20is%20a%20rare,to%20difficulty%20eating%20and%20breathing

Karp, H. (n.d.). Safe sleep and SIDS prevention. *Happiest Baby.* https://www.happiestbaby.com/blogs/baby/sids-prevention-guidelines-aap

Karp, H. (n.d.). Using the 5 S's for soothing babies. *Happiest Baby.* https://www.happiestbaby.com/blogs/baby/the-5-s-s-for-soothing-babies

Kids n K-9s, (n.d.). Dog bite statistics for the United States. *Kids-n-K9s.* https://kids-n-k9s.com/dog-bite-statistics-for-the-united-states/

Mayo Clinic. (n.d.). Solid food: How to get your baby started. *Mayo Clinic.* https://www.mayoclinic.org/

healthy-lifestyle/infant-and-toddler-health/in-depth/healthy-baby/art-20046200#:~:text=The%20American%20Academy%20of%20Pediatrics,-feeding%20or%20formula-feeding.

Mayo Clinic, (n.d.). Sudden infant death syndrome. *Mayo Clinic.* https://www.mayoclinic.org/diseases-conditions/sudden-infant-death-syndrome/symptoms-causes/syc-20352800

National Fire Protection Association. (n.d.). Tamper-resistant electrical receptacles. *NFPA.org.* https://www.nfpa.org/Public-Education/Fire-causes-and-risks/Top-fire-causes/Electrical/Tamper-resistant-electrical-receptacles

Sexton, S. & Natale, R. (2009). Risks and benefits of pacifiers. Mailman Center for Child Development, *American Family Physician,* 79(8). https://www.aafp.org/afp/2009/0415/p681.html

World Health Organization. (2012). WHO recommendation on bathing and other immediate postnatal care of the newborn. *WHO.* https://extranet.who.int/rhl/topics/newborn-health/care-newborn-infant/who-recommendation-bathing-and-other-immediate-postnatal-care-newborn

IMAGES

Figure 1: Sikkema, K. (2019). Baby's pink panty [Photograph]. *Unsplash.* https://unsplash.com/photos/If7eM-f7Ehg

Figure 2: Grossen, T. (2018). Siblings forever [Photograph]. *Unsplash.* https://unsplash.com/photos/zduBtIqdLls

Figure 3: Spanic, D. (2020). Baby boy [Photograph]. *Unsplash.* https://unsplash.com/photos/PC37Wo9QXLQ/info

Figure 4: Sikkema, K. (2019). Woman holding baby beside man smiling [Photograph]. *Unsplash.* https://unsplash.com/photos/WvVyudMd1Es

Figure 5: Romansa, A. (2016). Person holding baby's finger [Photograph]. *Unsplash.* https://unsplash.com/photos/5zpojym2w9M

Figure 6: Braun, L. (2020). Woman in black and white floral tank top carrying baby [Photograph]. *Unsplash.* https://unsplash.com/photos/82KmKGNteuo

Figure 7: Pham, K. (2018). Baby laying on bed while woman massaging his back [Photograph]. *Unsplash.* https://unsplash.com/photos/9nC7j1gAS84

Figure 8: Blum, B. (2018). Toddler wearing white tank top near white wall [Photograph]. *Unsplash.* https://unsplash.com/photos/d-RwmHvHPP

Figure 9: Streetwindy. (2020). Boy in blue and white polka dot shirt [Photograph]. *Unsplash.* https://unsplash.com/photos/iUVAe7gxAvw

Figure 10: Oslanec, P. (2018). Selective focus photography of sleeping baby [Photograph]. *Unsplash.* https://unsplash.com/photos/Mu6RjGUzrQA

Made in the USA
Coppell, TX
31 March 2021

52716093R00132